For Sal and Anne-Marie—

A Brief History of Innkeeping in the 21st Century

By

Shawn Kerivan

Very cool people... even if you're not innkeepers

ALSO BY SHAWN KERIVAN:

Name the Boy: Short Stories
The Vermont Press

Creative Writing in the Real World:
A Reader for Writers
New Plains Press

Iago's Fool
Auberge Books

A Brief History of Innkeeping
in the 21st Century

Shawn Kerivan

THE
VERMONT
PRESS

Stowe, Vermont

The events and situations described and depicted in this book are real. Some names and locations have been changed to protect the innocent and dissuade the litigious.

The Vermont Press
Stowe, Vermont 05672
Thevermontpress.com

The Vermont Press is a curated collective of independent publishers that offers innovation in storytelling and distribution through authors who write with clarity, velocity, humor, and a sense of social consciousness.

Innkeeping Innsights columns are reprinted with the permission of the Stowe Reporter.

Printed in the United States of America
First Print Edition

ISBN: 978-0692270257

Library of Congress Control Number: 2014948077

The text of the narrative is composed in Hoefler.
The text of the columns is composed in Courier.

Cover art by Taylor James.

Table of Contents

This book is dedicated to anyone who has ever...

Rolled out of bed at 1 a.m. for eighty bucks...

Cheerfully marched through the breakfast room
while holding a plunger...

Been reviewed by an illiterate expert...

Wrung body fluids from the sheets...

Or made lifelong friends
with people who pay to stay with you.

You're living the dream, my innkeeper friends.

<u>Introduction</u>

We were brand new innkeepers when it happened. It was bound to happen; there was really nothing we could have done about it. I think my wife and I had each individually prayed that it wouldn't happen, because it was so frightening. How would we handle it? Would we be okay? Or would we crash and burn, another statistic along the small business superhighway to hell. There was only one way to find out: we had to answer the bell—the bell at the front desk.

Just before Thanksgiving of 2000, my wife, Chantal, and I became innkeepers in the northern Vermont ski town of Stowe. But after a couple of weeks we still hadn't had our first guest. There were bookings for Christmas, but the first week of December was quiet, and we were surprised when the door jingled and two women walked in.

Not being used to the life as innkeepers, this unexpected home invasion startled us, mostly because it happened right in the middle of dinner. Little did we know that one of the curses of innkeeping is that most business is transacted during the supper hour—or when you're trying to take a shower, or when you're helping your kids with their homework.

We went out to the lobby and stopped. The two women regarded us from just inside the door. We returned their uncertain gazes. All that was missing was the theme music from The Good, The Bad, and The Ugly. Finally one of the women said, "Do you have any rooms?"

Rooms? Rooms? Do we have rooms? What an odd question. We hesitated. Then it hit us: we were innkeepers, this was an inn, these women were travelers, and they wanted a room. We had rooms. The simplicity of the situation astonished us. Yes, we had a room. A nice, clean room, with two double beds. And it was only $59, plus taxes and gratuity. Please follow me.

I remember thinking, This is going to take some getting used to.

Saying that innkeeping takes some getting used to is like saying that marriage takes some compromise. At our essence, we humans are clannish; it's a survival technique. And if you're not part of the clan, you're suspect. This instinct needs to be bred out of the innkeeper. Lots of people who aren't of your clan—unless your clan comprises every credit card-wielding traveler between Montreal and Philadelphia, between Boston and Beaver County, Pennsylvania—share the space under your roof. It takes some adjusting on your part, but then again, think of the travelers. They have no idea what they're getting into by checking into a small, eclectic inn. We thought we were the ones taking a big chance by buying an inn, but we had a lot to learn about our spot in the greater scheme of innkeeping.

§

There were no guarantees of success or happiness; there never are.

From the outside, it can look idyllic. From the inside, it can be harrowing. In that respect, innkeeping is like every other endeavor. Nobody goes into this business—or any other—with the knowledge that eventually they'll fail. But nobody goes into this or any other business with all the knowledge they'll need to succeed. And that definition of success, that critical mass of expectation, can be just the thing to sink the dreams of any aspiring innkeeper. Change will happen, and the speed and timing and sheer dumb luck of how one reacts to that change will often dictate success or failure.

But if success is a moving target, what's the best way to hit it? It's a complicated question to answer, more so for innkeepers who are really selling a piece of themselves, a piece of their personalities. The very notion of innkeeping is fully steeped in quaint emotion, and while that formula may have worked in the days before the Internet, now it's a new world. A bad review from a guest can make it around the world before the next morning's coffee is brewed. The image of the retired couple stocking an old Victorian with antiques and listing themselves in a few guidebooks is long gone. Modern innkeepers are lean, mean, marketing machines; competition is fierce. Because more people have the flexibility to choose innkeeping as a lifestyle, there are more inns around to keep. And because travelers can book rooms on their cell phones, in their cars, while they're on their way to their destination, the innkeeper has to be a high-tech geek or geek-ette.

And yet it can work. Imagine choosing a beautiful place to live and raise children, a place where you meet people from all over the world, a place that provides you with all your needs under one roof—imagine that place, and you've imagined the joys of owning and living in an inn. Take a couple of ski bums like my wife and me, and stick us in the Ski Capital of the East, and you get an idea of just how addicting this way of life can be.

But is there more? Can there be more? And what if you achieve success? What comes next? A promotion to a bigger, shinier inn? And if the threats to your way of life come from directions you never imagined, can you handle them? After nine years as innkeepers, we've seen a panoply of disasters, including droughts, floods, miscreants, crooks, recessions, bureaucrats, and family turmoil. Our biggest challenge may lay ahead of us, in the form of a market that threatens to upscale itself right out from under itself, while the national economy tries to implode. We'll just have to handle those challenges the way we've handled all the rest of them, and in the meantime, I'll write my way through it.

§

Somewhere near the end of Chapter Three I talk about my encounter with the Stowe Reporter, the weekly newspaper of our village. This book exists in part because of that encounter. In the spring of 2001, the publisher of the Reporter, Biddle Duke, invited me to create a regular column about life as a small, struggling innkeeper. We called it "InnSights," and for the next year and a half it ran every other week.

The columns were a way for me to reconnect with my writing, which—due to jobs and kids and inns—had fallen out of fashion. But the columns were also a way for me to explore and discover what it meant to be an innkeeper—or, as I soon realized, what it meant to be the innkeeper's husband. That contrast between my role and my wife's role, between my life inside the inn and my life outside the inn, became the central theme of not only the InnSights columns, but for this book.

The InnSights columns are collected in the Appendix of this book. They follow, more or less, the narrative of the chapters.

<u>Chapter One</u>
The Lightning and the Lightning Bug

If there's one thing I've learned as an innkeeper, if there's one thing that will stay with me forever, if there's one thing that defines the world of an innkeeper more than anything else, it's this: people are hairy.

It was a stunning revelation, an epiphany that lived at the heart of all my angst. When I figured it out, when I fully understood its implications, I was finally able to stop suffering the slings and arrows of outrageous fortune and take up arms against an oppressor that had been tormenting my life as an innkeeper for years. I was finally able to articulate the scourge of all innkeepers, the thing that ruins our lives and makes us miserable. The reason hair drives innkeepers bonkers is because we can't control it. We can wash sheets and towels, scrub bathrooms, paint rooms, raise our rates, turn the heat down, give advice, cook eggs, pour coffee—but we can't control the tiny, invisible hairs that float off people, orbit the earth for a week or two, then settle on a freshly laundered pillow case just before the next guest checks in. It's maddening.

After all the evolution, after all the improvements in depilatory techniques, grooming tools, and plucking devices, we human beings are still fuzzy. And worse than that, we shed. We shed like golden retrievers in June, losing great clumps of fur that choke bathroom drains and permanently attach themselves to bedding. We lose hair from every part of our bodies, from our shining skulls, from ears, from the knuckles on our toes, and everywhere in between. There's no end to the variety of hairs launching themselves from our corpses and settling into every crevice, every nook available in one of my guest rooms.

And the complete removal of hairs from a room is impossible. It can't be done. No matter how hard you try, no matter how diligently you slam your Oreck or your Dyson around the room, you can't suck up all the hairs the last guest left behind. Forget it. And here's another universal truth: hairs can't be seen until you're trying to check a guest into a room. Then, after hiding since the last feeble cleaning attempts earlier that day, they explode into the open, manifesting themselves with sudden violence, like bird crap on a windshield. They dance before you, mocking your discrete misdirections while you try frantically to pinch them out of sight. Finally, you realize it's impossible. You understand that you're not going to get all the hairs the last wooly buggers left behind, because guest rooms can't equal the clean rooms of IBM's chip manufacturing section. Guest rooms have people staying in them all the time, and people are hairy.

Here's a little test for you: The next time you're at one of those swanky, three-hundred-dollar-a-night luxury places, pack a penlight and get down on your hands and knees. Do some investigating. See what you can find. I guarantee you'll discover hair. It's everywhere, and nobody can do anything about it. Because when you let people into a room, the first thing they do is shed. It's almost like they open a barbershop. Sometimes I pause after I leave them, listening for the sounds of shears snipping. Snip, snip, snip. The sound of hair piling up, hair I'll never be able to fully remove from the room.

Oh, I've had twisted fantasies about trying to get the hair out. Everything from renting a power sprayer and coating the room with depilatory cream to buying a negative-pressure blower and sucking the air—and the offending hairs—out of the room. I've even thought of requiring guests to shave themselves smooth before check-in, but I stopped short of that. After all, how would I enforce it? Besides, they'd never be able to rid themselves of all their hair; they'd forget their noses, or ears, or some other hair-sprouting crevice.

If it sounds like I'm obsessing about hair, you're right. But it's not just hair I'm obsessed with. It's cobwebs and dust bunnies and those little, tiny corners you can't reach, where the floorboards meet, that get all grimy, and the only way to clean them is to swab a Q-tip with alcohol and put a headlamp on and crawl down there and scrub. But it's useless. Because tomorrow someone else is going to check-in to your inn, and they're going to track mud around, they're going to spill soda on the table, and worst of all, they're going to shed.

But I digress.

§

Welcome to the Auberge de Stowe B&B in Stowe, Vermont. I'm Shawn, and I'll be your innkeeper. Actually, that's not true. I'll be your innkeeper's husband; my wife, Chantal, is the real innkeeper around here. What's the difference between the innkeeper and the innkeeper's husband? Well, as Mark Twain once said, it's the same as the difference between the lightning and the lightning bug. In other words, all the difference in the world. The innkeeper's husband is the great man behind the greater woman. He's the guy who crawls around under the house when the pipes freeze. He's the guy who answers the call with a plunger in hand (after someone else has already answered the call). He's the guy who paints, chops, brews, sands, stirs, plumbs, zaps, and hammers his way through an old inn.

In other words, he is—I am—a verb.

Before we became innkeepers, I never would have guessed that such a docile looking occupation could be so...active. And I'd like to confess right away that I watched the television show Newhart faithfully for all those years. I even watched Fawlty Towers, and I never saw either of those innkeepers doing the things I've done. I never even saw Bob Newhart take off his cardigan. John Cleese got a little dirtier, but that wasn't always about grease.

I'm digressing again. It happens a lot when you're an innkeeper—or an innkeeper's husband. Digression is the natural state of progression in the innkeeping business: one step forward, two steps sideways. You go to do one thing, and three other things pop up. Try to change a light bulb and you're likely to find yourself at the hardware store buying a sump pump. Mowing the lawn leads to bathroom plumbing. Even saying "Good morning" to a guest can be tricky. As in, "Good morning," which evokes this reply from your paying guest: "There's no hot water."

Like the hot water heater that conks out in the middle of a busy winter weekend, the inn—and the innkeeper's husband, for that matter—are digressions themselves. You set out to do one thing, and life happens, and you end up somewhere else. We set out to be innkeepers, and while we still are, lots of things happened during the journey. Especially to me.

I wasn't always like this. I wasn't always focused on human hairs and ailing hot water heaters. Okay, I'm lying—but just a little. Deep down inside, I'm a neat freak, I'm an order-seeker, mostly because there's no order inside my head, and I need all the external structure I can get. Some people join the military to get their exoskeleton; I rearrange my sock drawer. But owning an inn pushed me over the edge, because now I didn't have to be neat for myself. Now I had to be neat for every single person that came through the front door. If people walked in and saw me sitting in a pool of my own filth, they probably wouldn't stay.

What I am focused on is helping Chantal run a good inn. Actually, let me widen that a little. I'm focused on being a successful business person. My aim is ensure that our little inn, the Auberge de Stowe, does the things we want it to do. For us, that means more than making money. For us, that means access to the kind of lifestyle we want, the kind of living we want. But at the same time, that means doing all the things that make a business successful on a monetary level, too. It means welcoming guests and making them feel comfortable, at home. And there's nothing that will kill an inn's business faster than dirty, hairy rooms.

I'm not a natural at this, and I've struggled at times with my identity, with my true purpose, because at my core, I'm a writer. And being a writer is not always easy to admit. But thanks to the patience of my wife, I've been able to incorporate my dream of realizing my potential as a writer with our dream of becoming innkeepers. It took some faith, especially on my part, but when I was finally able to say, "Hi, I'm Shawn, and I'm a writer," life improved. I didn't magically start publishing everything I wrote, but an alignment happened within me, a sort of compass needle reckoning that pointed me in the right direction—or at least served as a reference point.

The great thing about coming out as a writer was that I did it in France. Chantal was born and raised in France, and shortly after we met, we moved there, got married, and Chantal took a job with Sodexho, a multi-national foodservice company. I was free to write and tool around Alsace and the Vosges mountains on my bike. And when I was introduced as a writer, the French took me seriously.

"This is my husband, Shawn, and he's a writer."

Grave looks spread across their faces. My measure was taken.

"Ah, vous etes ecrivain. C'est bien, ca."

In France, not everyone is a writer. In France, not everyone is "writing something." Writing is still considered a métier, a vocation. There's training involved, commitment. I've always found it funny how so many people write books in America, yet most authors aren't writers. That's why France is such a good place to write, and why it will always be a good place to write. Not because you can sit at a Parisian bistro and drink strong, short coffees all day and write unmolested, and not because the pastoral French countryside is inspiring; France is the best place to write because writers are taken seriously. If you admit to being a writer over there, you better have the goods to back it up. You better not say something like, "Oh, I'm writing a book about my last bowel movement, or the company I just sold." You better be serious. And that might be the most important lesson I acquired while living there: I was a writer, and I was going to take myself seriously.

But that doesn't explain how we got here, innkeepers in a northern Vermont ski town. That seed has its roots in two places: the Blue Hills Ski Area in Canton, Massachusetts, and Ireland.

§

Rising to an elevation of over 600 feet, and plunked firmly within the Route 128 beltway that surrounds metropolitan Boston, the great Blue Hill is a funky little ski area that serves as greater Boston's learn-to-ski destination. During good winters, when the area is blessed with abundant natural snowfall, Blue Hills becomes a wonderland, a skier's gem tucked between suburbia and metropolis. On off years, the place won't open for long stretches, and operating a ski area a few miles from the ocean where winter low temps average in the low 40s can be more than a challenge. 8

One year, the winter of 1989-1990, I was a ski instructor at Blue Hills. And it just so happened that year was an epic snow year, and I skied 109 days in a row. Chantal, who at the time was graduate student at UMass-Boston, was also an instructor there, and as so often happens when true ski bums meet, love steps in to cement the deal. Skiing has always been one of the biggest parts of our lives together, and it started on a sunny day on a snowy hill within a few miles of downtown Boston. Through the years we skied as much as we could, including the Alps in both France and Switzerland, Mt. Tremblant in Quebec, and assorted New England ski areas.

The Ireland part of the story happened in 1992. We were living in France, and decided to make the pilgrimage. The first week we cycled around the Ring of Kerry. Each night we stayed in a different B&B, run by someone named Mrs. O'Sullivan. The entire peninsula of Kerry is populated by kind, severe ladies named Mrs. O'Sullivan, and they all run B&Bs. The precision and professionalism these Mrs. O'Sullivans displayed with their innkeeping inspired us, giving rise to the Mrs. O'Sullivan Method of Innkeeping: clean, comfortable rooms, affordable rates, and memorable interactions with the innkeepers.

It was actually Mrs. O'Leary, in Cork, who gave us our first taste of the frank, honest kind of innkeeping we'd later adopt for ourselves. We were about to set off on our bicycles for the Ring of Kerry, a sixty-mile trek, and it was pouring rain outside. When we told Mrs. O'Leary of our plans, she was aghast.

"Oh, you'll never make it. Will ya?"

We assured her that we were young enough and stupid enough to make it.

"Ah, well, ya better eat up then. More tea?"

Mrs. O'Leary's skepticism delighted us, even eight hours later when I was changing a flat tire in a downpour, somewhere near Kenmare. The rest of the trip went the same way: honesty and caring on the part of our innkeepers, reckless decisions and pints of stout on our part. The experience left us with a sense of individuality, for each place had the personality of the owner on it, each was unpretentious and unique. What a great way to live, we thought. And since we'd both stayed in B&Bs while skiing, the two ideas cross-pollinated, creating a new, original notion in our minds.

Then, it lay dormant for seven years.

§

Just as there's a huge difference between the innkeeper and the innkeeper's husband, there's a huge difference between thinking about becoming innkeepers and actually doing it. For us, that meant seven years of toying with the idea while life unfolded in spectacular glory around us: We moved back to the States, bought an old two-family house near Boston, had a baby, moved to Montreal, had another baby, and moved back to Boston in 1998. By then Chantal had left her job with Sodexho to stay at home with our sons, and I'd taken a job with FedEx to bring home the health insurance. But the idea of owning a little inn still lived within us, and thanks to the Internet, we were able to do something about it.

We had begun looking for inns online while we were still in Montreal. Though the Internet was still in its toddler-hood, realtors had quickly realized the power of the medium, and they were fully involved, even back in the mid 90s. And since Chantal and I didn't have a deadline or a specific goal in mind, we were free to dally across the globe and indulge different scenarios. We thought about the French Alps. We thought about the Rockies, in both Canada and the United States. We thought about New Zealand. We thought about Maine. In fact, we thought about almost every place that had great skiing. But we never thought of Vermont.

For the three years we lived in Montreal, we would drive home through Vermont, along Interstate 89. Each time we passed through, Chantal and I would notice how beautiful the state was, with thickly forested mountains plunging into trout-choked rivers, heavy snows in the winter, lush green growth in the summer. And we always said to each other, "It would be nice to live in Vermont, but it's just too expensive." So we carried on with our search, traipsing from one end of the earth to the other on dial-up speed lines at the Fraser-Hickson library in our Notre-Dame-de-Grace neighborhood in Montreal.

After we'd returned to the States, and I'd established myself with FedEx as a courier, we re-ignited our search for inns. By the spring of 2000, we were becoming serious. One the things driving us was the booming housing market in Boston. The two-family we'd bought six years earlier had now doubled in value, and we hadn't made a mortgage payment on it. By living upstairs and renting out the bottom unit, we'd been able to have our tenants cover the rent and taxes, allowing us to accrue 100% of the equity. Now properties were selling within hours of appearing on the market—some sold for more than the owner's asking price. Chantal and I realized that the timing was right: the real estate market was cooking, our sons were still only 6 and 4, and, most importantly, I could transfer my job with FedEx, which would allow us to keep valuable health benefits. It would also give us extra income, which would be important in our first few years as innkeepers. We'd suddenly turned a corner, going from dreamers to serious shoppers.

We knew the kind of inn we wanted (precisely), and we knew where we wanted it (generally). It had to be an operating inn that was under-marketed and ready to make the leap into the Internet age. And it had to be near a ski area—but not just any ski area. Since we were looking at smaller places—8 to 10 rooms, maximum—we needed a place with three-season draws. That meant skiing and winter sports, as well as fall foliage, and a strong summer season. And if we were looking in the States, it had to satisfy one other criteria: proximity to a FedEx station. Keeping my day job with FedEx was integral to our business plan. Most big ski areas fit our needs, but we didn't confine our search to New England. We looked to the Rockies, to Alaska—but now, with the FedEx Imperative, we had to confine our search to the States.

Most of the inns we saw advertised were higher end, turnkey operations. Those were exactly the kinds of places we didn't want. We wanted a place that had been around for a while, but needed an injection of new ownership. A place with some history, a place we could grow into. Having attended the University of Maine, I was pulling for Sugarloaf or Sunday River. But there was another wild card in our equation. We wanted somehow to incorporate Chantal's French culture into the operation. Ideally, that would mean a place close to Quebec—or in Quebec.

And then, in June of 2000, while Chantal was searching through the real estate listings, she came upon a property that seemed to fit all our needs. The broker listed a place called the Bittersweet Inn for just under three hundred thousand dollars. It had eight guest bedrooms, came with two acres of land, and it had no Internet presence. But most importantly, it was located in Stowe, Vermont. With its billing as the "Ski Capital of the East," Stowe and the slopes of Mt. Mansfield more than satisfied our ski bum's need. Vermont's reputation for foliage gave us big seasonal potential through October. And a little more research—thanks again to the Internet—revealed that the summer season was actually the busiest season in Stowe, with August bringing more visitors than any other month. But Stowe had more than that: it was a major destination for the Boston, New York and Montreal driving markets. There were 25 million people within a five-hour drive of Stowe. Plus, it was a 35-minute drive from Stowe to Williston, Vermont, where FedEx had a station I could transfer my job to.

We called the broker and scheduled an appointment to see the place. On the last weekend of June, we found ourselves pulling into Stowe, our eyes as big as saucers. The real estate agent representing the sellers was a retired Army colonel named Bob Evans. In his mid-70s, Bob had the energy and enthusiasm of a 20-year old. When he greeted us he was dressed in red chinos and a floral print shirt—hardly the garb of a retired Airborne warrior, but that was a theme we'd find repeated over and over in Stowe: people weren't there because they wanted to appear to be something; they were there because they were comfortable with who they were.

Bob showed us the place and did all the usual realtor things: talked about opportunity, the potential of the land ("You could build storage units on this land and make a fortune!"), and walked us through the entire inn. What we saw was an old, historic roadside inn. The eight guest rooms were right out of the 70s: small black and white televisions, painted dressers, lots of twin beds. The plumbing was out of the 70s, too—the 1870s. I groaned as I looked at the plumbing, heating, and electrical systems. They looked exactly like the systems we had in our two-family back in Boston: ancient, honorable, and ready to retire, most likely on my watch.

But the most appealing feature of the place had nothing to do with its business potential. It was the owner's quarters. The inn was a brick foursquare with a long wing attached. The wing housed the guest rooms; the brick building was the owner's quarters, and it was basically a separate house. This was important to us because we'd be raising a family, and we wanted our own home, not just an apartment carved out of an inn. We'd seen plenty of places—all of them online—that had cramped owner's quarters, and we eliminated them all. But this place looked livable, with a separate entrance, bedrooms, living room, dining room, and kitchen. By the time we piled in the minivan and headed home, we were very excited.

After talking with a friend back home who was a realtor—and who we'd retained to list our property—we emailed Bob up in Stowe with an offer. Counter-offers and counter-counter offers were made—all via email, while we sat in our jammies, sipping coffee—and by August we had an agreement. We also had an offer on our Braintree property. Things were moving fast, and it looked like we were going to be innkeepers. Or so we thought.

Chapter Two
What's in a Name?

First, the future innkeepers were going to school.

In a moment of logical brilliance, we'd written a training session into the purchase agreement. We figured that since we had zero experience as innkeepers, we should get some insight from the knowledgeable sellers. After all, they'd been at the innkeeping game for fourteen years; it would be arrogant of us to pass on an opportunity to glean some of their skills. So in late October, after the foliage rush, we headed up to the Bittersweet Inn to spend some time with the sellers.

Paul and Barbara Hansel were in their 70s, and more than ready to retire. They had been running the Bittersweet since 1986, and now some fairly serious health concerns motivated them to get out: Paul had a heart condition and Barbara was nearly blind. They were going to California, where they had some family, and they were going to soak up the sun and leave the toilet cleaning to some new blood. Despite any afflictions they may have been suffering, they were both robust and focused when we met them.

Paul was a tall, lanky man, a former engineer who had been integral to bringing municipal water and sewer service to much of Stowe, including the Lower Village, where the Bittersweet Inn was located. In fact, being on town water and sewer was a huge selling point for us. It relieved us of two major concerns that just about everyone else in Vermont was responsible for dealing with themselves: well water and septic fields. It would be one kind of hassle to have interior plumbing problems; most of those I could handle. But it would be quite another to have to deal with that stuff outside the walls of the house. Once you get outside, you begin to talk about excavating equipment and four or five digit jobs.

So while Chantal spent some time with Barbara learning the domestic side of things, I followed Paul around while he showed me some of the ropes—and peculiarities, and quirks, and secret handshakes—around the Bittersweet. When Chantal and I reconvened later in the day, we were surprised—not at the task that faced us, or the amount of work or knowledge innkeeping entailed. Rather, we were surprised at the behavior of the outgoing innkeepers.

The Hansels seemed peeved at having to satisfy our request for some training. What seemed logical to us appeared to pain them. As I followed Paul around the place, I asked him questions, mostly about systemic stuff: What does this sub-panel control? What's the procedure for pool maintenance? How often do you have to go to the dump? His answers were vague and dismissive: Some of the lights down here, you'll figure it out, whenever the barrel is full. Chantal had a similar experience with Barbara. We'd obviously misread the situation.

We were relying on our research, and all our research told us to request a training session with the outgoing innkeepers. This advice was predicated on the assumption that the outgoing innkeepers were happy to be outgoing. Clearly, the Hansels weren't happy. Was there lingering anger about the negotiations on the selling price of the inn? Were there personal issues within their family? We could only guess. But it didn't make for a textbook entrée into innkeeping, and since textbooks were all we'd had to prepare us, we faced an uncertain transition.

§

Uncertainty followed us back from Vermont to Braintree, Massachusetts, where the agreement we had to sell our property there fell apart. The potential buyer, our neighbor, suffered a personal setback when his wife was diagnosed with cancer. Facing uncertainty himself, he withdrew his offer, and we were left owning two places in two different states at once. More importantly, we needed the money from the sale of the two-family to apply toward the mortgage on the inn. Things were getting dicey.

One place where things were not getting dicey was at FedEx. In September I told my manager that I'd be leaving, and that I wanted to transfer to Williston, Vermont. By chance, one of the operations managers I'd worked for had at one time been the senior station manager in Williston. He picked up the phone and called Vermont, and a few weeks later a position was posted. While the position was an unglamorous split-shift delivery/pick-up route, I jumped on it, knowing how important the FedEx job would become once we were innkeepers. My first day of work in Vermont would be Monday, November 22. Now all we had to do was sell our property.

Much to our relief, when we put the two-family on the market, we had three offers—two of them over the asking price—within a few days' time. And that was the moment when we knew there was no turning back. We were cutting our ties with the old world, my home, and we were committing to something bigger than ourselves, bigger than our lives. We were committing to a dream. We moved to Stowe on November 20, 2000, and that night it began snowing. It didn't stop until the following April. It was a good time to transition to innkeeping; November is the height of stick season, a low time for visitors, a time for hunting and hunkering down as the first snows blow in. We moved in, and the new innkeepers and the quiet inn began learning about each other.

We had a new name for the place: Auberge de Stowe. Auberge is a French word meaning "country inn," and with our location so close to Quebec, we hoped to capitalize on the potential French-speaking tourists that poured into Vermont. Calling the place "Auberge" had a lot going for it: the above mentioned draw for the Quebec market; the reflection of our family's French heritage; and it was a name that began with the letter "A," which meant it would be near the top of all the B&B listings, electronic and otherwise. (This was the pre-Google age.) One drawback with the name was pronunciation. People struggled to say it, even after they heard it: oh-BARE-je. But when we discovered the name, Chantal and I felt it was so right for us that we'd stick with it. If we lost business because some people couldn't deal with the name, we'd make it up with more business somewhere else.

Naming your new business is one of the most exciting things you can do; it's rivaled only by naming your children. Chantal and I adopted a relaxed, lengthy approach to choosing the name. We would each jot down ideas, then come together and compare what we'd had. And before we settled on Auberge de Stowe, we plowed through dozens of other possibilities. At first, I favored place names, descriptors that would reflect the geography, things like Cady Hill Inn (Cady Hill was right behind us) and Little River Inn (the Little River flows through the back of the property, on its way to the Winooski River and Lake Champlain). There was never a question about renaming the place. We both thought that Bittersweet wasn't the kind of name we wanted for an inn. It seemed to invoke too much contrast for potential visitors, as if they'd had a great time staying with us, but contracted food poisoning from the omelet we served. So by the time we got to "Auberge" we both realized how perfect it was, despite its potential drawbacks.

Now that our inn had its new name, it was time for us to make it our own. Chantal got to work on creating an Internet presence, beginning with a website. The traditional forms of advertising—guidebooks, brochures, listings—were becoming obsolete fast. By the year 2000, more and more people were using the Internet to plan their vacations. It was the best, low-cost kind of exposure we could have. We had another resource for business, too. The local business association in Stowe, called the Stowe Area Association (SAA), drove customers to lodging establishments by offering a central reservation system. Potential visitors could call SAA, and a representative would match them with a place to stay. For a little place like us, it was like having our own full-time staff of travel professionals.

And little we were. With eight modestly priced guest bedrooms, we occupied Stowe's vanishing affordable accommodations niche. Much of the town is filled with high-end, luxury places, resorts like the Stoweflake and Trapp Family Lodge, and posh inns like the Stone Hill Inn. Looking up and down the listing of small inns and B&Bs revealed only a few in our range. There was the Burgundy Rose on the southern edge of Stowe; across the street from us was Dick Brackenberry's Stowe Bound Lodge, a throwback with bathrooms down the end of the hall; halfway up the mountain road was the Riverside Inn; and a few more scattered in and around the village. If you wanted to come to Stowe during Christmas week and wanted to spend under a hundred dollars a night on a room, your choices were few.

§

During our first weekend, we set about exploring the place. The Auberge was part of a building dating back to 1835. Situated on Vermont route 100 a half mile from Stowe's village center, the Auberge had been an inn of some kind for more than 40 years before we arrived. Before it was the Bittersweet Inn, it had been called the Lower Village Inn, and before that it was the Brick and El, a name that invoked the structure. The original building was a brick foursquare design popular in the early 19th century. With its Cape-style roof and red-brick exterior, the building was one of thousands like it found throughout Vermont.

Judging by the newer-looking foundation under the el (an "el" is a section of a building longer and narrower, often used for connecting a barn to the living structure), the long wing running off the brick portion was probably built in the 50s or early 60s. Most of the guest rooms were located in that portion of the structure.

The rooms and the layout reflected the unique nature of the Auberge. Each room was different in shape and location, and none matched the others. Room 1 was directly off the lobby. With two double beds and a huge, true divided light picture window, it was a bright, roomy place. It also came with a funky bathroom featuring a big, pink toilet and an aging shower stall. Perhaps the strangest thing about the bathroom was its awning window that opened out to the back guest living room.

Leaving the lobby, you come to the breakfast room. Situated on the back of the house, the breakfast room overlooks the back property, two acres of lawn running down to a river, with Cady Hill rising up beyond. A converted porch, the breakfast room came with more awning windows, single pane, freezing in the winter. It needed a lot of heat to overcome the cold, but folks loved having their breakfast there because of the views.

Continuing along the back part of the el led to the back guest living room. The dominant feature of this room was he gigantic, sunken hot tub in the middle of the floor. It was a shade of brown called toasted almond, a color famous for its ubiquity in 70s-era kitchens. This water monster burbled under a ghoulish looking cover, and negotiating traffic around it was a challenge. It did provide heat to the back room, keeping the place almost tropical. After the back room, there was a hallway that led to a door far down the end of the el. On either side of the door were more rooms: 2 and 3 on the right; 4 on the left.

Rooms 2 and 3 shared a bathroom. Chantal and I never liked this setup. Not because sharing a bathroom with a stranger made us squirm (come on, we all share bathrooms with strangers every day), but because the rooms were side by side, and if you stayed there, you were really sharing more than a bathroom. It was connected to your room—your bedroom. If my delicacy is too subtle, let me phrase it this way: nobody wants to lie in bed and listen to strangers, ahem, test the plumbing. Or snore. Early on we tried selling rooms 2 and 3 as separate entities, but we soon abandoned that idea. Instead, we combined them into a two-bedroom suite, better suited to families. That eliminated the shared bathroom as an issue, as well as making the rooms more appealing to families, which was one of our stated goals going into this thing.

Across the hall was Room 4, the other room with two double beds. Located at the far corner of the house, Room 4 was bright and sunny and very warm—it was directly over the heating system. Room 4 gets a workout. It's convenient, affordable, and it has a nice, compact bathroom. Above it, up the stairs, was Room 5, and across the hall, Room 6. Those two rooms had more potential, but their biggest draw was that they were situated on the back of the house. Far down a long, winding hallway were Rooms 7 and 8. These rooms were actually located within the walls of the brick structure that was our house. They were a two-room suite, with two twin beds in Room 7, and a full in Room 8.

The place had its quirks, and there was a lot we could do to it. But first, we had to get through the winter. Then, we had to deal with the roof, which leaked everywhere.

The hot tub would have to go, and we'd need two new decks to replace the ones falling off the back of the house. That's the thing about buying an old inn and becoming an innkeeper: you always have more ideas than money.

§

While things seemed to be going the way we wanted them with the inn—our stuff arrived in a big moving truck the first week, and we were getting used to answering the phone in a business fashion—things were less obvious with the transition to my new job with FedEx in Williston.

I'm a big believer in intuition, and the moment I stepped inside that FedEx station—BTV, as it's known in the world of airports and express shipping—my heart sank. I knew I was in the wrong place. I'd come from a station that was growing and pulsing and exciting. I arrived at a station that was dour and miserable, where the plane carrying all of our overnight freight was late arriving almost half the time. I'd come from a place where working for FedEx wasn't seen as a stroke of good fortune, rather one choice among many. Here, in northern Vermont, a job with FedEx was a gift from the gods, because high-paying jobs for unskilled workers were almost nonexistent.

I didn't view my job the same way my co-workers did. For me, it was an instant strain, with a horrific schedule that kept me away from home, away from the inn, for 13 hours a day, while only paying me for 8 hours of work, due to the split shift I'd taken. Worse was the intense physical nature of the route I ran. Though I arrived in Vermont in excellent physical condition, my route covered several heavy stops, including two ski distribution centers, and an educational text printer. My truck left the building each morning groaning on its springs. It returned later that night in the same condition.

Worse, for me, was the feeling that I was abandoning my family. Chantal was left alone all day to deal with everything, for in addition to the regular family duties, we had a business to run. I'd leave for work at six-thirty in the morning and not return until nearly eight at night. The boys would be in bed already, and I'd be wild with hunger and exhaustion. As we entered December and guests actually began showing up, things ramped up at FedEx, for Christmas is that business's peak season. My days grew longer and more intense, and my physical exhaustion became a permanent state just as things got busy for Chantal at the inn.

Chapter Three
Thinking By the Numbers:
Innkeeping for Dreamers
and Bean Counters

Ignorance is the condition of being uneducated, unaware, or uninformed. And if business, and the freedom to create your own business, is the engine that drives America, then ignorance is the grease that lubricates that engine. Without ignorant dreamers, nothing would ever happen. While it's worth exploring the role ignorance plays in the human condition, its role for potential innkeepers is even more fascinating. As every inn and B&B is different, so, too, are the dreams innkeepers bring to this pursuit.

A few months after we'd moved in, we were at a gathering for local business people. It was a mixer, with everyone from innkeepers to lawyers to restaurateurs drinking free beer and wine, and noshing on complimentary appetizers. The purpose of the gathering was to cross-pollinate and build a stronger sense of community within the professionals of Stowe. For Chantal and me, it was our first chance to meet our neighbors. Not long after we arrived, a woman came up to us and introduced herself. She owned one of the larger motels in town, and had been in the business for many, many years.

"So, how are things going for you so far?" she asked through mouthfuls of guacamole. We mumbled something about adjusting, and we talked about how our first winter was going. Then we said that we hoped we could last as long as she had lasted.

"Hah!" she crowed. "Let me tell you something about this business. The people who make it are the ones who can last the first three years. That's your toughest time. As long as you've got a plan and someone with a job, you'll be okay. Ooh, is that shrimp? Excuse me."

Chantal and I looked at each other; we were too well prepared to claim ignorance. So we hoped that our numbers would add up, and we'd last through that critical first three years.

§

Our thinking was this: we don't know how to be "professional" innkeepers, so we're not going to try. And we're not going to bet all of our resources on a little roadside B&B. We looked at the numbers, we did the math, and we knew the occupancy potential. We compared those projections to our expenses, and by expenses I mean the mortgage. At the time, our mortgage was a little over $2,000 per month. The average room rate when we took over was $70 per night. Simply dividing the room rate into the mortgage would give us the total number of room-nights needed per month to cover the mortgage: 30. But everybody knows that the mortgage usually represents about a third of your expenses. (A third if you're smart; if you're a dope, it's up around a half. Anything more than that and you'll be one of the failed business statistics within three years.) That left us with a goal of about 60 room-nights to break even.

Okay, here comes more math. We had eight guest rooms, but really we only had six, because two were two-bedroom suites. While the two-bedroom suites represented more potential income, they were also harder to sell. Six rooms multiplied by 30 nights in a month equals 180 possible room-nights each month. Multiply that by $70, and you get $12,600 per month. When compared with projected expenses of about $4,000 per month, that seems great, right?

No. That $12,600 figure equals 100% occupancy. Nothing is 100% in this world—nothing. And even if we could achieve 100% occupancy, that would mean a yearly income of $151,200, leaving about $100,000 of profit annually, out of which you'll pay lovely taxes that will leave you with about $60,000, out of which you'll pay for things like your vehicle, your kid's braces, etc. Oh, and I didn't even mention that at 100% occupancy you'll need to hire help, because it's not humanly possible to turn over every room every night by yourself, so deduct another $10,000 from that, plus the added wear and tear from being that busy, system breakdowns, replacement of durable goods, probably another ten to fifteen grand, and now you're down around $35,000 per year.

But there's no such thing as 100% occupancy over the course of a year. The industry standard is about 35%. The really great innkeepers are up over 50%. We've had months where we touched 50%, and it was hellacious. And it takes years to get to 50%. So, being a super optimist, cut in half all the numbers above. But not really. Cut it by a third, and an accurate picture of what goes on in this industry emerges.

Here's how that occupancy standard translates to Stowe. Let's start in the winter. We're close to full on almost every weekend in the winter. Notice I said "close to," and "almost." Those are innkeeper words. I borrowed them from the fishing industry I grew up in. Ask an innkeeper how the weekend was and she'll say, "Great." Ask a lobster fisherman how he's doing and he'll say, "Slammin' them." Right.

But during winter weekdays, we're almost always empty. Oh, we get the occasional room-week for someone on vacation, and during the holiday week of late February we're booked solid, but that's it. Then comes the next season, which used to be called a "shoulder season" because it shouldered between winter and summer. It's more accurately called "mud season" because in the spring, everything turns to mud in the North Country. It's April and May and the beginning of June, and it's a long time of haphazard occupancy. In all our years of innkeeping, our occupancy hovers around 10 to 20%. Then comes summer, where we might be full on Wednesday night, but not Friday night. August is the busiest month in Stowe, and occupancy goes over 50%. It's a good month. Almost as good is fall foliage, but that's shorter, starting about mid-September and lasting until Columbus Day. After that, in November and early December, everything stops. If the snows are late, there's nothing until Christmas. Old innkeepers have told about how they used to survive. One innkeeper said that people would call in late October and reserve for the Christmas holiday. Back then, people would mail checks up as a deposit. Innkeepers would cash the checks immediately. The desperate ones would pay off some of their bills; the successful ones would fly to Florida for Thanksgiving.

That's the picture for the Stowe area, and Stowe is one of the best places on the planet to be in this business. We have three guaranteed seasons: summer, foliage, and skiing. Within those seasons we have guaranteed 100% occupancy weekends or weeks, with lots of events to draw people. In the summer it's the annual antique car show in August. In the fall it's Columbus Day Weekend. And in the winter it's Christmas week and President's Day and the week that follows.

In their excellent book So - You Want to be an Innkeeper, Mary E. Davies, Pat Hardy, Jo Ann M. Bell and Susan Brown offer some comprehensive and often exhaustive numbers to think about. They advise potential innkeepers to plan occupancy by cutting in half the first year occupancy, with 10% growth year over year, until you reach the area standard occupancy.[1] That means that if you're not in Stowe, or some other tourist Mecca that pumps visitors up the road, plan on half whatever their average occupancy is for the first year of operation.

While the numbers don't seem encouraging, few of us make decisions based solely on the numbers, which is why the business failure rate is rivaled only by the divorce rate in America. We're optimists; there's nothing we can't do, and even when we fail, we spin that failure to make it look like something natural that we'd planned all along. Chantal and I came to innkeeping with a slightly different regard: we were prepared to fail.

Perhaps this is a more European outlook, and perhaps the strapping Americans reading this are curling their lips with disgust, but it's a great thing to know all the eventualities, to anticipate them, to be prepared for them. Call failure whatever you want, but we all deal with it ever day of our lives. When the military fails it's called tactical realignment. When a baseball player fails it's called "batting .300." When a parent fails it's called "Do as I say, not as I do." When an innkeeper fails it's called "Looking for new opportunities," or, "We're so busy, we're just burned out." Sure, whatever. If that's what it takes to keep moving forward, to stave off the demons of disappointment, then that's okay. But Chantal and I choose what we believe is a healthier approach to that part of life. We embrace it as an experience, an opportunity to learn, to live, to share.

So there we were, in the summer of 2000, sitting down with the banker, proposing our modest business plan, with the full knowledge of all the numbers cited above dancing around our heads. We must have been crazy. How could we possibly NOT fail? We were looking at an earning potential of about $50,000 per year, after three to five years of operation. And why would a banker loan us the money to do this? I think bankers might be the biggest optimists of all Americans, and that's a good thing. As a nation, one of our defining characteristics is that we'll tolerate failure if it contributes to the independent character of the citizens. Without that tolerance, we wouldn't be Americans. But the banker needs his pound of flesh, and he's not necessarily interested in taking over an inn when the innkeepers fail. So we brought four things to the table that the banker liked a lot.

The first was money. Bankers love money not because they're greedy, but because it's their business, and the more money they can cycle through the bank, the more money they make, and the more successful they are. It's their commodity, the thing they trade to make a little profit on. We had money. Not only did we have the money from the sale of our two-family in Braintree, but we sold at the top of the market. The Internet bubble would burst in 2001, aggravated by the events of September 11, and the housing market would fall all over the country. But in the summer of 2000, it was smoking right along. We sold our house for something above our asking price, and that number was twice what we'd paid for it six years earlier. Add to that the fact that the mortgage had been paid for over that time by the tenants' rent, and we walked away with a nice profit.

We needed that profit, because things aren't cheap in Stowe. It's significantly costlier to buy into the game here, and even though we were getting a great deal on our inn (motivated sellers), the place needed a lot of work right away, which would eat into our cash stash. We also knew that we'd have to live off that money for a while, and that sobered us up.

The second thing we brought to the deal was my job with FedEx. Our banker wanted to see income that could be used to pay the mortgage he was offering. I was able to show him a $30-40,000 per year income (depending on the number of hours worked) right off the bat. He liked that. It meant that even if we didn't rent out a single room, there'd be money coming in, money to pay his mortgage. The importance of having an outside job going into this cannot be overstated. It reminded me—and perhaps this is where I internalized this business truism—of something my father said about lobster fishing.

After several years as a lobster fisherman, my father left to become a carpenter. In the end, he just couldn't make it fishing. He always told me that there were two things that made a successful lobster fisherman, and you had to have both in the beginning. The first was an innate ability to know where the lobsters lived, and to drop your traps right on top of them. But the second was more revealing. He said that all the successful lobster fisherman he ever knew had a wife who worked outside the home. That income, meager though it might have been, sustained the lobster fisherman and his family through the tough months and years that constantly plague that industry. That income allowed the fisherman to keep making payments on his boat, to keep learning how to become a better lobster fisherman. And that lesson wasn't lost on me. I was to be the innkeeper's husband, the one with the sustaining outside income.

The third thing we brought to the banker was our business plan. It was modest and realistic, and it assumed none of the optimism normally associated with a start up business. Maybe this disappointed our banker. Maybe he was one of those super banker optimists, and he wanted to see a pie-in-the-sky plan full of fireworks and parades. Or maybe he was quietly impressed that we'd thought this thing out so completely. The final thing we presented to him was potential. Not the inn's potential, but Chantal's potential. In the event of total failure, Chantal—who holds an MBA and has years of experience at high levels of the hospitality industry—could go back to work. We could, if necessary, close the inn as a business, live there as if it were only our home, and pay the mortgage, as well as our other expenses. Deal done.

If it seems like we had everything under control, if it seems like we'd thought through every eventuality, and were prepared for everything from wild success to abject failure, it's only an illusion. Here's the truth: until we opened our doors, until we started serving breakfast and making beds and cleaning toilets, we weren't innkeepers. And success? What really defined success? Was it simply money in the bank? That wasn't what we were after. Though underneath our funky Vermont quilt there lay an exhaustive financial plan, we were still dreamers and misfits who didn't share most of the conventional dreams of our family and friends. We didn't want to fail financially, but we weren't necessarily looking for that kind of success, either. What we were looking for was something not found in a spreadsheet, something detached from a tax bill or a mortgage. We were looking for a way of life that matched our spirit of openness and satisfied our curious natures, and we hoped to find it in a little roadside inn.

Chapter Four
A Winter of Discontent

Help was on the way.

My wife's mother, Trudy, moved in with us just before Christmas. Freshly retired from nursing, Trudy was a domestic trouper, and would be invaluable to Chantal, especially as we sorted ourselves out that first winter. She could snap a sheet into a hospital corner and wield a bucket of soapy water with the best of them, and we were grateful to have her. As it turns out, she arrived just in time in more ways than one.

One day, during the first week of January, in the middle of a frigid, dark stretch of winter, it happened. In the middle of my delivery route, my back snapped. It felt as if a firecracker had gone off in my spine, somewhere between the shoulder blades. I was immediately immobile; any movement caused sharp, anguished pain. I radioed the station and limped home. I was sent to a doctor who examined me and who winced every time I cried out. He prescribed horse tranquilizers and sent me home.

My upper thoracic area was on fire. When I got home, I put a huge ice pack on the couch and lay squarely on it. In an hour I'd melted through it, and needed another. I could move none of my upper body, and breathing was difficult. Finally the happy pills kicked in, and I drifted off. But there was no improvement the next day. Massive doses of anti-inflammatories only made Uncle Inflammatory jealous. I was writhing in pain, and I was pissed off.

I'd complained to my manager about the route I was working on several occasions. But to my dismay, not only did my concerns go unheeded, more stops were added. And after the injury, I was informed that FedEx was holding me responsible. In other words, it was my own damn fault that I got hurt. I must have done something wrong. While the ramifications of that decision were only slight and long term (it would affect my review, and my ability to pile on those cost of living raises that FedEx was so generous with), it really broke my heart. I held FedEx in high esteem, and I didn't come to work there because I had nothing else to do. I'd admired FedEx and the people who worked there, and I believed in their philosophy of the Purple Promise.

But now I was a pariah. And to make things even more uncomfortable, the doctor I'd been sent to couldn't diagnose my problem. His frustration bordered on unprofessionalism when one day he blurted out, "There's nothing I can do for you. You're going to have to go back to work whether you like it or not." Eventually, a CT scan was ordered, and when that revealed nothing, I finally got a referral to a chiropractor. Meanwhile, my first winter at the Auberge disappeared under an endless parade of ice packs while I occupied the couch.

It killed me to have to watch Chantal do everything herself, and rely on her mother for the rest. At least when I was at work I didn't see things that would upset me. But as a doped-up invalid the endless work of innkeeping unfolded before my eyes, and I could do nothing but watch.

When I finally started going to the chiropractor, things turned around. During my first visit he correctly diagnosed the problem. The muscles attached to the vertebrae had spasmed due to fatigue (big surprise), and they'd locked T1 through T3 together. The doctor manipulated my back, releasing a huge crack of energy, and for the first time since my injury—two months—I could stand upright. Over the next few weeks I visited the chiropractor twice a week, becoming stronger—and more euphoric—with each visit, until the middle of March, when I was cleared to return to work.

The experience changed me in many ways. First, it opened me up to chiropractors, a group I'd disdained in the past. What changed me wasn't so much the treatment as it was the philosophical approach to my injury. I felt like I was part of the solution, not part of the problem. The ordeal also opened my eyes to working for FedEx. I realized that injury was a real possibility, and that not all employees were exposed to the same level of risk. I'd done my stretching, used the approved lifting methods, and still was injured. On top of that, I was blamed for it. My opinion of my employer crashed. Add to that the guilt I felt about leaving the bulk of the heavy work at the Auberge to Chantal and her mother, and a neat platform of cynical misery appeared under my feet. That winter, heavy took on new meaning for us.

§

Like the pain that radiated out from the center of my back, the ancient asphalt shingled roof on the Auberge meted out its own kind of pain that winter.

The roof saga came as no surprise. When we first looked at the place, we saw a dying roof, sagging on its rafters. Having lived in the North Country before, in both Maine and Canada, I understood the critical role a roof played in building integrity. More than a shed for snow and rain was required up here. A roof had to be able to hold snow several feet deep, resist ice damming, and look good while lasting another 30 years. Replacing it wasn't sexy, and it wouldn't rent us rooms, but it would release us from the misery we endured that first winter.

The roof that came with the building held the snow. But when it rained on top of the snow (and it rains on top of the snow every year up here), water trickled down, exploiting the shingles that had worn out. That water found its way down through the ceiling, where it dripped into the breakfast room and the back guest room. Buckets bloomed across the floor and the sound of dripping beat out a rhythm.

We discovered another problem with the roof in March when we received close to ten feet of snow. The old asphalt shingles didn't shed the snow. It simply built up and threatened to collapse the building. Since I was still suffering my back injury, Chantal was forced to get up on the roof and shovel some of the snow off. Shoveling snow off the roof is common in Vermont; it's also one of the most dangerous jobs around. After serious snowfalls, hospital rooms and headlines are full of people who fall off roofs and injure themselves. I was glad when April came around and it finally stopped snowing. Our water problems didn't end, though, because the ice dams that formed on the roof allowed the water to crawl back under the shingles and turn the inn into a tropical rain forest. I couldn't wait to see that roof gone.

Actually, the old shingle roof's still there. But now there's a metal roof about two inches above it, installed over a strapping system that renders the metal roof "cold." This means that the roof doesn't receive any warmth from the building, which inhibits ice dams from forming, and that leads to a new problem: keeping the snow on the roof. After snow builds up on the metal, it comes off like an avalanche. In some spots we've installed snow brakes to hold the snow back long enough for it to come down gently, in small drops. But in other places it comes off like a glacier calving.

The roof issue that first winter illustrated something that required a more structured approach to the problem. While positioning a plant underneath a dripping ceiling in the back room might have been a creative solution, it was only temporary. Replacing the roof removed most of the issues we had with water, but not all of them. Because as lovely as snow is during the winter months, in the spring, it all turns to water. As good as the old roof was at pumping water into the house through its leaks, the new roof was better at shedding that water to the ground. And once that ground was saturated, the water targeted the house—at the basement level. We soon transitioned from emptying buckets in the living room to using a wet vacuum to suck water out of the lower level.

At the front of the inn, the front door is protected by a porch roof. Next to the front door are the stairs leading to the laundry room with ski storage. Beyond that is the finished basement area that had become our boys' bedroom. One of the quirks of the old building was that the grade ran in reverse from the parking area out front. This meant that any melting water or rain that couldn't be absorbed by the ground—like, say if the ground was frozen, or if there was a feet of snow—would run back down those stairs, into the laundry room and, if there was enough water coming from the sky, into the finished bedroom.

One night that first winter, after we'd had our twenty feet of snowfall, I arrived home from FedEx, tired and miserable. I went downstairs to the boys' room to kiss them goodnight—it was after eight and they were already in bed. I took a step onto the carpet and heard a squishing sound. Brendan, at the time only four, said, "Dad, I can see your footprint." I could see it, too, until it filled up with water. The room was inundated with water pouring in from outside. I scooped up the boys and plopped them in an unoccupied guest room. Most of the rest of the night was spent listening to the roar of the wet vacuum, until its motor burned out. Chantal and I gave up after that and went to bed.

Sometime in April, when guests stopped showing up and giving us money for accommodations, when the rain and melting snow threatened to float us away, we looked at each other and questioned our hasty decision to do this, to buy an old inn and try and live as innkeepers. I was stuck in a job I hated, a job that wore me down day after day, a job we needed not only for the income, but for the access to health insurance it provided. Chantal was trying to get a struggling business off the ground and raise two boys. Our building was falling apart around us, and we feared no amount of monetary injections would revive it. The steel gray skies continued weeping into May, pausing only for a snowstorm on Mother's Day, which seemed a fitting insult to our pathetic trajectory.

Why would we stay?

§

The answer came not in any anecdote, not in any epiphany, but in scores of small events, the kinds of everyday blessings normally overlooked unless the torque of stress lights them. In April my friend Pete came up for a few days of skiing. It was my first real time off in a year, and the dynamic of getting out of bed in the morning and being on the slopes in 15 minutes wasn't lost on me. For the first time I had a taste of why we were doing this.

And did I mention it was April? Unless you live somewhere south of Virginia, you understand why T.S. Eliot reviled it in his epic The Waste Land, where he talks of zombified lilacs and amnesia-inducing snow.[2] Nasty stuff, April. With more than a twist of irony Eliot captured the state of mind of Northern Vermont in April. Still longing for winter, cherishing the muting cover of snow that insulates us from the world, we long for that comfort, because with the effort of coaxing a few tubers and lilacs out of the ground, we're completely spent. It's a time of culling. But not this April. This April—at least the week Pete came up—was sunny and mild, a rare gift of true spring skiing.

We skied recklessly through thickets and copses that lashed our faces beside the trails. We rode chairlifts that dangled through tunnels of snow. So great had been the snowfall that season that shovel brigades were dispatched to dig out half-pipes beneath the lifts. Even so there were places where my skis—and Pete's snowboard—grazed the top of the snowpack, its glistening surface some twenty feet above the ground. The skiing wiped away much of the misery of FedEx, the back injury, the financial worries, and the uncertainty about the future—at least for a week. That was the power that skiing held over us.

§

After six months in Vermont, I was finally starting to slow down.

If I was driving behind someone who wasn't doing the speed limit, my blood pressure didn't skyrocket. If a contractor didn't show up at the stroke of 9 a.m., I didn't plot his assassination. There was a river running through my backyard. I could fish anywhere—I rarely caught anything, but still. Hiking opportunities abounded. If we wanted to go on vacation, we opened the back door, and there it was. Cliché though they sounded, living in Vermont offered us all those things. Being innkeepers satisfied some deeper urge within us. It was an urge to keep control of our lives while ministering to others. While we could have just stayed where we were in suburban Boston and done any number of charitable things, we never felt at home there. For me, that was difficult, because that's where I'm from. But the place had become toxic to my writing and to me— or maybe vice-versa—and finding our way in Vermont became the most natural thing in the world. While renting out guest rooms is strictly a business arrangement, on another level it's not. It's taking care of somebody, assuming responsibility for them for the night—or three nights, if it was a good booking.

The cycle of booking a room when someone calls, greeting them when they arrive, making them feel welcome, providing them with comfortable quarters, feeding them, and cleaning the room after they leave, was like a short story to me. Its duration was relatively brief. Each guest was completely different. There was a beginning, middle, and end. Every reservation became a complete dramatic action, and each guest became another little story.

And as I thought more and more about that analogy, I began to think more and more about my writing. Way back in my mind, I thought that innkeeping would lead to more writing opportunities for me. I pictured myself someday just writing and innkeeping, cranking out books and making beds. The future I saw for myself had no FedEx in it, no getting up and 4:30 in the morning, no driving up snowy and icy country lanes to deliver another sweater from L.L. Bean. And while I didn't have a sharply defined vision of my future, I knew what it didn't look like.

My writing had been on hiatus for several years, and things were starting to get backed up. After recovering from my back injury, I was back at work full-time, which meant leaving early and getting home late. Though the weather had moderated into warm, sunny days, I still felt trapped, and I knew that summer would be the shortest of the seasons in Vermont; winter lurked behind every cool night and fresh breeze.

So I started looking for another job.

Chapter Five
Under Pressure: Water and Blood

That first year, I ended up sneaking around a lot.

This was something I became used to after owning an aging Victorian two-family in Braintree, Massachusetts. Every creak, every tick of a heating pipe, every drip ignited my senses, because the consequences of a sound out of place could be dire. A creaking floorboard could mean an intruder; a random drip could signal a pipe about to burst; the soft hiss of the steam heating system—or, the absence of the soft hiss—could mean total disaster. It was much the same in the old building housing the Auberge.

For me, going to bed meant lying down for six hours with my eyes wide open and my ears on high alert, listening. Mostly I listened for the peal of smoke detectors, but the other thing I listened for was weather. Our first winter had treated us to the phenomenon of rain on top of sleet on top of snow, which meant a flooded basement. So I'd crane my ears and strain to hear the unnatural sound of rain against the window, and plan another hasty retreat from the basement for the boys. It was just one of many things that could roust me from bed and send me sneaking around, investigating with pessimism.

One night I heard a sound that I couldn't immediately identify because I hadn't heard it in a few years. It was a light clicking noise, as if someone were gently manipulating the delicate bones of a skeleton in a velvet bag. It was uneven and irregular, and when I went to the window I saw it: ice.

Our last run-in with ice had come in Montreal in January, 1998, and it had been courtesy of the Ice Storm, the one that turned Quebec into a Cormac McCarthy novel: desolate and remorseless. Back then, the ice had laid waste to the countryside, destroying the power grid, sending us fleeing from our city apartment for ten days. After that experience, we were twitchy whenever we heard there'd be rigid precipitation coming from the heavens. So when I saw ice collecting on the window, I thought the worse.

Then I heard another noise: the low rumbling of a diesel engine, followed by the zing-zing of tires on ice. The sound came from our back parking lot, so I snuck around to the back door and peeked out. I saw running lights, and they were red. Being a boy of the sea, I immediately thought I was looking at the port side of a ghost ship, a long lost vessel that the Bermuda Triangle had dropped at my doorstep. Then I could make out the set of double-dually rear tires mounted on the hind end of a box-shaped whale: it was a bus. What the hell was a bus doing in my parking lot spinning his tires at ten o'clock at night?

I trudged out to find a bus driver standing alongside his vehicle, scratching his head. The bus was sideways in the lot, and we could see that it would be going nowhere without a tow truck. He told me he had a reservation with us, so we went inside, and I wondered aloud where we were going to fit the 80 people who rode up in his bus.

"No, it's just for me," he said. "The rest of them are staying across the street at the Commodore's Hotel.

"Wait a minute," I said. "You're staying here with your bus, but everyone else is at the Commodore's?"

"Yup. Can we go in and call a tow truck?"

That illustrates how our first winter as innkeepers went. Everybody else got the bookings, while we got the bus that had to be towed.

§

In Vermont, winter turns to summer on May 15th.

My father always said, "Up here, March and April are winter months." It was true, and that knowledge mitigated the pain of April. But nothing prepares you for May in Northern Vermont. It's agonizing. Buds are on the trees, grass is trying to grow, and you can even feel the sun—sometimes, when it decides to come out. But for the first half of the month, purple clouds blot the sky, rain erupts in slashing sheets, and it usually snows on Mother's Day. Not enough to cover the ground, just enough to make you cry.

But then, overnight, about the middle of the month, everything changes. You wake up one morning and there's a softness to the sounds outside. The songs of the birds have a little more breath beneath them. The apple tree sends out pale pink blossoms. Peepers erupt nightly. You can feel the entire earth relax and loosen.

And that's it. Winter is suddenly over. That day, temperatures will reach into the mid-70s. People stand outside looking stupid, dazed. Everybody knows that they made it, they survived another winter, and now it's summertime. Within a week every tree in the state will have exploded green, a frothy, iridescent green that nearly glows in the dark. The sun comes out, stays out, and everything begins to steam. The state liquor store sells out of gin in a day. That night, people will sleep with their windows open.

The consequence of this season-change is water. And it turns out that water is a bigger concern to innkeepers than just about everything else. In the winter, it's frozen water that turns the village white and coats the slopes with frozen gold. In the summer, water fills the streams, luring fisherman and canoeists and kayakers out to play. Water fills our hot tub and cascades from out showers and shimmers in our pool. But water also has a dark side, an insistent, uncontrollable mandate that turns it from benign accompaniment to subverter of profit. In April and May, water melts, and it falls from the sky, and it pushes on the little inn from all sides.

Our first run-in with water came courtesy of the hot tub. The story of the hot tub, and how it evolved into its current, outdoor form is bemusing. When we bought the inn, it came with a "spa." Our working knowledge of a spa comprised images of people being massaged hairy, ham-fisted men. So we were surprised to see a huge, burnt-toast-colored sunken hole in the back room.

The only way to describe the indoor hot tub that came with the inn is...70s. Everything about it, from its color to its indoor location, screamed double-knit, reversible slacks, platform shoes, and hairy chests. It occupied more than half of the space in the back room, a twelve-by-twelve portion of potential living area surrounded by tropical plants whose mid-winter existence could be directly attributed to the bubbling humidity issuing forth from the 500-gallon water source.

I hated it immediately. It was ugly and tired looking, and it showed signs of wear that were irreversible. For a cover it had a piece of foam insulation that floated on the surface. The color of the tub itself was fading in spots. And there was my own prudish attitude toward hot tubs. Aside from the notion of climbing into a vat of simmering water that's been incubating everyone else's body flotsam before you got there, there's the whole image of hot tubs, which in my mind were suitable only for hairy California hippies.

Though I never liked this model, my attitude toward hot tubs softened considerably that first winter. It happened when I suffered my back injury at FedEx. The doctor recommended whirlpool therapy, and when I told him about the big beast in my back room, he encouraged me to use it. The first time I stepped into it, a soft heat raced up from my feet, liquefying my inhibitions. As I settled into the water, all the discursive thoughts I'd harbored toward the beast swam away. I was so relaxed I nearly drowned. I quickly became hopelessly addicted to its curative effects.

But that didn't help save the hot tub. It became a real estate question, and the real estate in question was the back room, and our plans for it. Having a hot tub burbling next to the only small table and chairs guests had to use was, in our opinion, not conducive to our vision for that area. The room had big, beautiful windows looking out over the back of the property, and we saw the hot tub space as a guest living room, with a gas fireplace, television, couch, chairs. There was also an energy consideration. The hot tub was fired by a propane boiler the size of a Bunsen burner. Hardly efficient. The only question was how to do it—how would we get that thing out of there?

Fortunately, it tied into our larger plans. That first spring, we hired a local contractor, Tommy Fletcher, to build three new decks and put a metal roof on the place. There'd be a new deck off the back guest living room, and we asked that it be built with enough strength to support an outdoor hot tub, which we intended to buy that fall. It was clear to us quickly that guests loved the notion of a hot tub, and even the big, brown beast got plenty of use. Whenever someone called up to book a room, one of the first questions from them was, "Do you have a hot tub?" The second question was, "Is it outside?" For us, the next step—buying a new hot tub and installing it on the new back deck—was a formality.

So we asked Tommy if he could make the hot tub disappear and replace it with a floor that I could finish off and add a living room on top of. Armed with a reciprocating saw and a three-pound sledge, Tommy reduced the old, fiberglass hull to a pile of memories. The new floor went on top of the old space, and a gas fireplace went in, and the place looked cozy, even if it was a little chilly on the coldest days. But that was a project for another time.

§

The Auberge is a true roadside inn.

For thousands of years, accommodations were offered to travelers wherever they made their way in the world. Not coincidentally, these establishments blossomed alongside the road, where the travelers were. Only recently has the phenomenon of "destination B&Bs" crept into our lexicon. But the essence of innkeeping remains deeply engrained into the commerce of the infrastructure. The Auberge is no different.

While we're perched in Stowe's Lower Village on Route 100, the property behind the inn slopes down across two acres of lawn to the Little River. On the other side of the Little River is River Road. For most of the year, the river is nothing more than a shin-deep stream, bouncing from one bank to another, gouging out an occasional pool deep enough to hold a couple of trout, as it flows into the Waterbury Reservoir, and eventually the big Winooski River, which itself dumps into Lake Champlain.

This innocuous flow has a malevolent side, too. In the spring, when the snow melts off Mt. Mansfield and the surrounding peaks, the river swells, rising up its banks.

And if heavy rains conspire with ice damns downstream, that little shin-deep trickle can get mean enough to float a car. Or worse, jump its banks. In the eight years we've been here, I've never seen that happen. But the neighbors—and previous owners—have. And that's why our two acres of lawn, with the pool and the shed, are in the flood plain. And because that land is in the flood plain, it's good for nothing except mowing in the summer, and building snowmen in the winter.

Not that I'd want to build anything down there. But those thoughts do cross a boy's mind from time to time. I mean, I think a couple of tastefully built townhouses would fit in nicely in that space. But I'm getting ahead of myself. I also think a community garden would be great, too. But it's not going to happen. All of that land is within the 500-year flood line, which comes right to the base of our stairs. The 100-year line comes to about the halfway point of the land, effectively rendering the land nothing more than a pleasant view. Once again, we were done in by water.

I don't think the effect water has had on our experience can be overstated. In the natural world, sun is life. And I suppose that it's so for innkeeping, too, for without the sun the rain comes, and rain is water. But water's importance is beyond proportion in this business. It is both vital and vindictive to our chosen field. From the plumbing to the pool, water takes precedence. Think of it from the innkeeper's point of view: if a guest comes and says a light isn't working, you go and change the light bulb. Or you tell them there's a power outage, which is beyond your control. But if someone says there's no water available to flush a toilet or take a shower, you're in trouble. A tree may fall on a power line, or a scheduled power outage might happen in the middle of a busy week, but plumbing is the innkeeper's responsibility, and all the leaky roofs and wet basements in the world won't take the place of a nice, hot shower.

§

My sneaking around wasn't confined to the inn; that winter, I looked just about everywhere for a job other than FedEx.

It was late spring, and like all other life forms in northern Vermont, I was trying to shake off the winter lethargy. FedEx was helping, working me to the bone. All the toxins ended up in my sweat-soaked shirt each night. And so I began looking around for some other kind of work. But, I wondered, what would I be qualified for? In college I'd majored in broadcasting, and I'd worked in television and radio for a little while after, but I didn't like it. Since then I'd been a carpenter, painter, ski instructor, energy auditor, and I'd worked in the commercial fish business. Though I didn't see anything that spoke to me in the area, I still felt I needed to leave, to move on, if only for my own health and sanity.

From a logical standpoint, this made no sense. At FedEx I was making fourteen dollars an hour, my comprehensive health benefits cost us under a hundred dollars a month, and I could work as many hours as I could stand. As I began to search for a job, I realized that replacing that package would be impossible. But I was determined to change things, cost benefit be damned. I had a lot of faith that Chantal could turn this place into a profitable operation.

The places I checked out ran the gamut of opportunities around here. I applied for a job as a maintenance technician at the Golden Eagle Resort. It was a full-time position, and it came with benefits, but the pay would be about forty percent less than what I was earning at FedEx. Still, I reasoned that the quality of life would more than offset the reduction in income. Working two minutes from home would be a great comfort to both Chantal and me.

I also applied for a job as a reporter for the News & Citizen newspaper in Morrisville. Though I had no credentials as a reporter, the manager liked my writing samples, and the interview went well. Again, pay was an issue; I was offered about $300 a week for a full-time job, and that didn't include reimbursement for all the driving I'd be doing.

I had another idea. The local paper, the Stowe Reporter, was advertising for a new beat reporter. Again, experience was the main obstacle, but I knew I was a good writer. I also had an idea for an article, or a series of articles, about innkeeping. So I sent something in to the editor, then followed up with a phone call. He really liked the piece I'd written, but he didn't think it was right for the paper. He urged me to pitch him some more stories, though, and I was encouraged by that. But that still didn't solve my FedEx dilemma.

So I decided to force the issue. I went to my senior station manager and told him I had two other job offers (the Golden Eagle and the Morrisville newspaper), and that I was prepared to leave FedEx. I knew I was in a good position, because it takes almost three months to hire someone and get them trained as a courier. At the time, the unemployment rate in Vermont was low, and I knew that FedEx was short-handed. So I told my senior manager that I wanted to shift from full-time to part-time, mornings only.

I took him by surprise, and he seemed genuinely concerned about the reasons for this decision. I also showed him the two job offers, and I told him I was prepared to become unemployed if neither worked out. I also told him my first choice would be to stay with FedEx; that was only half true. There was nothing I would have liked better than to walk away from FedEx. I'd known from the moment I walked into the BTV station that I was in the wrong place. In my mind I continued to argue that if I got a part-time morning position my troubles would mostly go away. But my heart knew better. My heart knew that I didn't want to drive out of Stowe every morning and load and unload containers of freight, then hustle to the airport, then hustle back to the station and jump in a truck and deliver packages all morning. What I wanted to do was sit in my breakfast room and sip coffee and write words.

But that would have to wait. The senior manager agreed to my request, and within a month I was a part-time, morning courier. It was a big step in the right direction. Now I was home between noon and one in the afternoon, and I could really help Chantal. And, just as importantly, I was around to see my kids in the daylight hours. I was there when they got off the bus. It was the kind of life change that allowed me to open up and begin to embrace the true nature of my spirit as a person and an innkeeper.

Chapter Six
Ferrymen, Circus Performers, and Innkeepers

I'm not really sure when I became so reverent, so spiritual about this whole thing. And by "this whole thing" I'm not sure if I mean life, or baseball, or innkeeping, or some blend of it all. Maybe it was the simple act of spending more time as an innkeeper, and less as a courier. Whatever the cause, faith crept in, wrestled me away from my secular sight, and restored the mystery to my life. And a belief in mystery is essential for survival, because not everything can be explained by Area 51 in the Nevada desert.

Telling people you're an innkeeper is like telling them you're a writer. Their reactions are similar and consistent: they always pause, and a bemused look comes across their face, a look that says, "Oh, yes, I've heard about that before." And then all the clichés begin to kick in for them. Some come right out and ask if I've ever seen Newhart, in which Bob Newhart plays a transplanted innkeeper. Since I lived in Vermont, many people knew an innkeeper already, so I wasn't looked on with quite such exotic eyes. But the identity began to grow into me, changing my essence.

The center point of any trade is cloaked in mystery, and this finally dawned on me after about six months in this business. That's how long it took for me to get used to seeing people come through the front door, as if this place were an inn, as if I were an innkeeper. After six months, I finally began to see things through the guest's eyes, to experience what they were experiencing. There was a time when I was out front, chopping wood for the fireplace, when some guests pulled in to the driveway. As they approached, I smiled and waved, said hello. They smiled back, but their smiles were different, more amused, perhaps a little wary. That's when I realized that I was holding an axe, wearing a plaid shirt, and standing in a pile of wood. I must have seemed so far from their reality then, and I think that might have been the moment I went through the looking glass. From then on I could see the other way. Why did that happen to me then? That's the mystery. That's the thing you can't write into your business plan, the thing you can't predict.

Art is a lot like that experience with the guests and the axe. You can't deliberately plan for the moment that something becomes art, or the moment you become the artist. But you have to be open to it. It has to be organic to you, or people will sniff you out. Fortunately, I never gave it too much thought, otherwise I might have been frightened off before I gave it a chance. Innkeeping is like any other cult: the greater the disingenuity, the greater the faith. That ignorance is important in the beginning, because it gives you access to the wonders of faith. And as you slowly shed the innocence, you become bitter and cynical for a while. You may wander. But the truth within you will bring you back. It always does.

There was a time during our first winter when my ignorance helped build some of that innkeeping faith. It was while I was recovering from my back injury, slowly rehabbing on the living room couch. One day, while I was happily dozing under the influence of Percocet, I heard footsteps in the dining room. Not the footsteps of my wife, however. These were heavy, booted footsteps, coming slowly toward my supine self.

It's worth noting that in Vermont, we have different notions of security from folks in other parts of the world.

There's an openness in Vermont that you don't find elsewhere. Stop by Mac's Market or the post office on a winter day, and you're likely to find three or four cars sitting unoccupied, idling, while their owners run inside. Though it's not environmentally sound to leave your car idling, it shows how secure people are with their surroundings. Many Vermonters think the safest place for your keys is dangling from the ignition, that way you never have to look for them. Combine that with innkeeping—where you're essentially begging people to invade your home—and you start to get an idea of how likely it is that someone would wander into my living room.

That's the mindset I had as I waited for the bootsteps to get closer that day. Maybe it was something nefarious, but I was doped up enough with Vermont and painkillers not to care. That's when a head peeked around the corner. The head was unkempt and scruffy, sporting an oily ball cap proclaiming either a beer's greatness or a race car driver's legacy; it was too dirty to tell. For a minute, the head looked at the television, which I think was tuned to ESPN. Then it looked down at me, stretched out on the couch.

"How you doin'?" asked the head.

The head's accent confirmed what I already knew: this was no potential lodger just up from Connecticut. There was nothing refined about the head's diction, nothing to

suggest an education at an ivied hall, or a life led in a genteel suburb. This was a local head, a working head, a head
that spoke the language of hardscrabble living. Somewhere
inside me, under layers of painkiller, concern flickered.

"I'm doing okay," I said. "What can I do for you?"

"I need a room. You got any rooms?"

"Sure. I have lots of rooms."

"I mean by the week. I need a room for a couple of
weeks."

"I bet you do."

While we were talking, the head turned away from me
and watched television, and only then did I feel the first
flicker of resentment. I could put up with someone coming
into my private space to look for a room, but don't watch
my television. Don't usurp my cable. I paid for that program, and I'll decide who gets to watch it with me.

The kind of annoyance I began to feel wasn't really the
kind you'd associate with a home invader. It was that
uniquely American kind of aggravation: it's mine, I paid
for it, you can't have it. I think it's interesting to see that
when my privacy and security were compromised, I was
tolerant. But when the sanctity of my cable television was
violated, I bristled. I wanted the head to know that, I
wanted the head to understand that one simply didn't
watch another man's cable television program uninvited.
The head chewed something and continued watching.

"So what do you think?" the head finally said, as the program went to commercial.

"I don't have any rooms by the week. Try the Pines down the road."

The head grunted, looked from me to the television once more and, seeing nothing about either beer or auto racing, withdrew. I heard the boot steps slowly fading, heard the door to the lobby jingle, then close. I waited a minute, then hauled myself up and staggered over to the window. A jacketed figure was walking away, back down the road, dirty hat matting a tangle of hair. I stayed there, leaning against the window, watching until the figure vanished around the corner. I could feel myself slipping into one of those contemplative moods that a writer friend of mine once described as "visiting." It happened when I withdrew from the matrix of the active world around me and descended—or ascended, I haven't figured out which one it is, yet—to a place where there's just me, and an idea. At that moment I was alone with the idea of a man looking for a place to live for a couple of weeks.

Because I'm a Catholic, I immediately felt bad about turning the man away. I felt like I'd violated the charity clause of my contract. Because I'm an innkeeper, I felt like a failure. But wasn't the situation clear? Here was a guy looking for a place to live for a few weeks. From his point of view, he does the logical thing: he stops at local lodging places—especially the ones on the road, like ours. I don't know his reasons for needing a place for a couple of weeks. I simply fall back on my training, and when we started out in this business, Chantal and I decided that we wouldn't accept boarders. That simply meant we didn't want long-term lodgers. But I couldn't shake the feeling that I'd let this guy, or someone else, down. That I'd had an opportunity, and lost it—and I don't mean an opportunity to make money. I don't think what I felt had anything to do with the medication.

It was our first year as innkeepers, and we were still learning, still experiencing new things, and this was one of them. For me, in my state of visiting as I watched the man walk into the cold, it was a moment of deep pondering, of reflection beyond myself. What had we tapped into with this choice of innkeeping? There seemed to be a larger force at work here, a historical precedence leaning on us. Was it possible that by luck we—as spiritual people—had stumbled on to something as artful as us? Was innkeeping more than just a business?

I'm great at wondering, and with the time on my hands to explore the background and philosophy of innkeeping, and how it might interact with our own personal philosophies and beliefs, I immersed myself into its history. It turns out that innkeepers have their own patron saint, St. Julian. His full title is St. Julian the Hospitaller, and innkeepers don't have him all to themselves. St. Julian is the patron saint of ferrymen, innkeepers, and circus performers. His patronage also includes the childless, fiddlers, jugglers, knights, murderers, pilgrims, shepherds, and wandering musicians. Like most of us, St. Julian is overworked and spread too thin, a victim of the world's demands for productivity. But his story, while clearly apocryphal, illustrates what we innkeepers are up against.

There are several histories of St. Julian, all with debatable facts, which only adds to the legend. My favorite rendering of his story comes from Gustav Flaubert. "The Legend of St. Julian the Hospitaller" ("La Legende de Saint-Julien l'hospitalier") appears in his book *Three Tales* (*Trois contes*), the last work he completed. In the introduction to the Alfred A. Knopf edition of the book, Harry Levin frames Flaubert within the confines of a tri-logical approach to his writing. He cites three of Flaubert's previous novels, *Salammbo*, *Saint-Antoine*, and *Madame Bovary* as examples of this treatment, where Flaubert examines the three periods of mankind: paganism, Christianity, and something that translates roughly as the bourgeoisie period. The theme is repeated on a smaller scale in Three Tales, with "A Simple Heart," "The Legend of St. Julian the Hospitaller," and "Heridious." St. Julian's story becomes a Christian fable, and what a fable it is.

Julian is born of wealthy parents, and as a child he's given everything, including love. He becomes skilled at hunting, but something's wrong with him: he begins to kill animals for the thrill of it. This addiction blossoms, and the body count rises, until one day a magnificent stag that he's just slaughtered at the end of a particularly bloody campaign prophesizes that he'll murder his parents. That's it for Julian; he renounces his ways, and goes on the road, fleeing from his parents so he'll never fulfill the horrible prediction. He wanders, survives only on the kindness of strangers (including innkeepers, which is how we ended up with him as our patron saint), then becomes leader of a band of fighters. Here he excels (remember all the hunting?), and he becomes a great warrior. His legend grows, his victories make him famous, and finally, as payment for saving his kingdom, the Caliph of Cordova presents Julian with his daughter as a wife. Julian settles down; he is happy.

But one day, the temptation to hunt overtakes him again, and he goes on a forest-clearing rampage. In the meantime, his parents have arrived at his castle after many years of searching for him. They're welcomed by his wife, who gives them her own bed to rest in. Later that night, Julian returns, his blood boiling from the day's killing. He sees two figures in his wife's bed, thinks she's betrayed him, and kills them both. But, of course, it's not his wife and a lover, it's his parents, and suddenly he's fulfilled the stag's prophecy. Again, Julian flees.

This time his misery is for real. He becomes a beggar, and tells his awful story to anyone who will listen. Soon he becomes infamous, and villagers board their doors when they see him coming. He is abused and repulsed and shunned by mankind. Animals, too, fled from his approach, for his murderous ways preceded him. He did heroic deeds, saving people from tragedy, and still was unfulfilled. His thoughts turned finally to suicide.

At the treacherous crossing point of a wild river, Julian finds the remnants of a boat. He repairs it, and decides to make the ferry his life's work. Soon travelers begin to show up, demanding transport. Julian charges nothing and suffers their abuses. Then, one night, in the middle of a storm, a leper hails him from the other side. Julian picks him up, takes him into the hovel of his home, and comforts him without protest. When the leper grips him tightly, demanding the heat from Julian's body, Julian obeys, pressing his flesh against the open sores covering the leper's body. Suddenly the leper's eyes become "bright as stars," and he grows to fill the entire room, imparting on Julian "an abundance of delight." With Julian still clasping him, "The roof flew off, the firmament unrolled—and Julian rose toward the blue spaces, face to face with Our Lord Jesus, who carried him to heaven."[3]

If that story demonstrates the requirements for saint-hood, I'm a long way off. I would have lost my temper with the jerks who abused me when I was begging. But I never suffered the kind of misery Julian suffered. More amazing is that Flaubert got this story from the stained glass windows in his church. It's safe to say that this story, like most stories of saints, received some embellishment and editing along the way.

St. Julian's tale, like most legends, offers redemption,. And while most innkeepers don't go to war or accidentally murder their parents in a jealous rage, there's something healing about this métier. To open your home to strangers is the most noble thing one person can do for another. It's been held up and taught to us, no matter what our culture or religion. Without hospitality, the world simply wouldn't work, because hospitality is at the core of humanity and civilization.

When I learned of St. Julian's story, I thought back to that day when I languished on the couch, and the stranger wandered in, looking for a place to stay. I realized instantly that I was no saint. But then again, Julian was trying to make amends for horrific deeds. His story shouldn't be used as a stick with which we beat ourselves. It should serve as inspiration and a reminder about the true nature of innkeeping and hospitality, for there are always great tragedies that await our heroism.

Shawn Kerivan

<u>Chapter Seven</u>
September 11, 2001

Around nine-thirty a.m. on the morning of September 11, 2001, at the FedEx terminal in Williston, Vermont, one of the Customer Service Associates called me over to her desk. She pulled up Yahoo.com on her computer and showed me a horrible headline: a plane had crashed into one of the World Trade Center towers. I remember thinking something generic at the time, distancing myself from the improbable, for it didn't seem real, it couldn't be real. For a few moments, the last few moments of the old world, I deliberately failed to comprehend what was happening. And then the second tower was hit, and we all knew we were in trouble.

It's not that it took that second tragedy to indict us. But it shook us hard and opened our eyes. And it stripped away any lingering doubt about us as a people, our place in the world, and our beliefs.

September 11 was already an important date for Chantal and me. It was our wedding anniversary. And that year, 2001, was our first as innkeepers. That should have made the day more special for us, and we'd planned a lovely dinner out at a French restaurant. We were approaching our first yearly cycle as innkeepers, with only fall foliage to negotiate before we put our first year in the books. We felt like we were finally getting our sea legs, finally setting down some roots in this community, finally doing something we loved, in a place we adored. And though we neither saw, nor felt, nor heard the terrible events taking place in New York, and Washington D.C., and Stonycreek Township, Pennsylvania, they reverberated through us, immediately, an echo refusing to fade away.

The first consequence we felt was the grounding of all domestic flights. That meant FedEx was mostly out of business. The company would be able to truck a certain amount of freight regionally, but the main business of flying packages was suspended immediately. It was a painful dilemma for the company. Customers were still open, still doing business, still shipping packages that needed to be picked up. But there was no place for anything to go. And there's one thing FedEx doesn't have: warehouses. They fly packages; they don't store them.

With volume drying up instantly, there was no work for part-time delivery drivers like me. In the short term that meant a couple of days off. But in the long term, I quickly realized what this kind of tragedy could mean for a company like FedEx. I knew we'd be allowed back into the air quickly, and the rumors said we'd be back up in two days. In fact, we started flying again that Thursday night. And since we weren't a passenger airline, we wouldn't suffer the consequences—whatever they turned out to be—that domestic carriers would suffer. But what kind of effect would this disaster have on the economy, if any?

That led to another consideration: what about the inn? We didn't have to wait long to find out. Within two days, we'd received a couple of cancellations. But as time went on, we discovered we were in better shape than other establishments in town. Because most of our guests drive to us, only a couple of folks called to say they just couldn't face getting on a plane. Other places—the bigger and the more upscale—had a larger percentage of guests who flew, and had higher cancellation rates. I'm not sure how they dealt with it, but we were very forgiving, forgoing the cancellation policy in an effort to respect the range of emotions involved.

The longer-term effects would play out over the winter, and beyond, but the one thing we had going for us mitigated our fears: we were already at the bottom, and if we could survive one year of it, we could survive another. As it turned out, by the morning of September 11, 2001, the economy was already in a recession, and had been since March. The bubble had burst, and nothing was left, except sticky gum on our faces. The debacle of Enron—poster child for the Decline and Fall of the Dot Com Revolution—was still off in the future. September 11 turned out to be not the debilitating blow to our economy and our way of life that the terrorists had envisioned. Rather, it was a punch that slipped through and knocked us on our arses, and surprised the hell out of us.

What we can never do—and weren't able to do that first night after the tragedy—is divorce the humanity from the tragedy. Because we, as Americans, have the ability to consider our fellow citizens as a special sort of kin, we all lost family that morning. We didn't need to see faces, or hear numbers. We'd been violated in an especially horrible way, on a national level, and on a personal level. Never again would Chantal and I be able to look at our anniversary without remembering the other reason the day is remembered. It was as if, in the sheer scope of their malevolence, the terrorists had found time and space enough to snatch away something personal from us, to smear it with the blood and screams of a horrified nation.

But, alas, there was one thing the hijackers may not have counted on: we're Americans, and if we're good at nothing else, we're the best at shrugging off tragedy and getting on with things, a trait endemic to a nation of immigrants. So, guiltily, we kept our appointed time at the French restaurant, partially because we knew the person that owned the restaurant was in the same situation as we were, and partially because it was an excuse to get away from the images pulsing at us from the television. But mostly we wanted to go out and be alone together, and think of that other September 11, the one that happened in 1993.

§

September 11, 1993, was actually the second time Chantal and I were married to each other. The first time was December 14, 1991, in the office of the mayor of the village of Brunstatt, France. We had moved to France the previous January, when Chantal accepted a position as marketing director for Sodexho in the Alsace-Lorraine region. Brunstatt was a small town southwest of Mulhouse, a large industrial city, home to a Peugeot factory, which in turn was the largest account for Sodexho in that region, and the reason the regional office was located in nearby Sausheim.

We'd decided to get married in 1991 for a couple of reasons. First, and most obvious, was that we were, and are, deeply in love with each other. After moving to France and living together, it became obvious that we were meant to be together. Beyond that, there were other advantages to being married, tax related and otherwise. Once married, I could apply for a work permit in France, and perhaps get a job. Though my job there was to become a writer—and I succeeded in having several short stories published, as well as writing several novels—I wanted to do more, to teach English maybe. So on a sunny, cold December day, accompanied by Chantal's godparents, who served as our witnesses, we went to the mayor's office, signed papers, nodded gravely to his serious inquiries, and rang the bell in the tradition of the region, announcing our union. We returned home immediately after, opened a bottle of champagne, and called everyone back in the States. Then we went out to dinner. Lovely, simple, and succinct. But not complete.

All along we'd planned a church wedding for when we returned to the States from France, because all along it had been our intent to come back. And when we returned in August of 1993, we had a month to find a place to live, buy a car, and plan a wedding. Fortunately, we invoked the same spirit of our first wedding day: simplicity. We were married in the Assumption Roman Catholic church in Green Harbor, Massachusetts, across the street from where I grew up, and we held the reception at the Green Harbor Yacht Club a mile down the road. The Yacht Club—which isn't nearly as pretentious as its name implies—sticks out into Green Harbor, home to hundreds of fishing and pleasure boats, all anchored calmly in the afternoon sun for our guests to admire.

That was the September 11 that could never be taken away from us, the day we remembered as we held hands at the restaurant the evening after the other September 11. Though we knew that we would never be able to think of our wedding anniversary in the same way again, we also understood the difference between the two dates. Plus, we had an alternate wedding anniversary, the December 14ᵗʰ date. And finally, we had a lot to celebrate that year. We had jumped in and bought our B&B, survived the first, awful winter, reeled under the crush of August traffic, and now the foliage bookings were coming in. We weren't setting any records, and we knew we'd be broke for a long time to come, but we were living in Stowe, skiing almost whenever we wanted, hiking, biking, canoeing, just enjoying one of the most beautiful places and dynamic towns to be found anywhere. That was the spin we put on it, the positive things we clung to as we clung to each other that evening.

Over the years, time has done what it always does. We don't feel any less grief at the calamitous events of 9/11, but we've learned to live with them. And we've learned to live with our anniversary, which should always be apart from anything else that happened on that day.

Chapter Eight
The Degrees of Faith:
What They Don't Tell You About
Time, Love, and Business

We humans love time. We love the concept of time, and that love expresses itself the way all true love does: by showing the complete range of emotion possible when devotion dictates behavior. We honor time by enslaving ourselves to its demands, by wearing little time disciples around our wrists, by displaying it in our vehicles, on our billboards, and on the towers of our churches. Perhaps the highest honor we bestow upon time is by lacing the clichés of our language with its image: time marches on, time and tide wait for no man, time is of the essence, killing time, time will tell, and, my favorite, *tempus fugit*, time flies. What greater honor could we give a cliché than to grow it wings and fly it off into the sunset?

Time, of course, is linked to the natural world. In Vermont, the passing of the seasons is so pronounced it's almost violent. For example, let's look at summer—and by summer, I mean meteorological summer, the warmest ninety days of the calendar year. In northern Vermont, those ninety days aren't all connected, they're not all in a row. In northern Vermont, summer comes around the middle of May, lasts for three weeks—during which time there are wicked thunderstorms, soupy humidity, gasping heat, and bright, green leaves budding from the trees—then it goes away. June is disgruntled, with enough cold and rain to remind me of my home, Green Harbor, Massachusetts, where June nor'easters lashed the coast with cold rain for days on end. Then, around the beginning of July, when everyone's worried the corn will never grow, summer returns. It stays hot for about six weeks, and there'll be a heat wave thrown in there somewhere. But about the third weekend in August, something changes. We'll wake up one morning and it will be more than cool outside; it will be cold, close to forty degrees. And for the next few days, the sunshine will only warm the temperature into the sixties. And that's pretty much it. Summer's over.

The first half of September will be warm, warmer than the end of August, but it won't be summer. The kids will be back at school, people will be more industrious in everything they do, and the sun will slant at a different angle, suddenly shining in our eyes when we head down South Main Street by the police station. Around that time of year, there always seems to be bits of shattered taillights on the pavement right around that spot, as if that new angle of sunshine induces fender-benders, and the fender-benders signal the change in seasons.

Even if we ignore the calendar, the seasons mark a repetitive cycle that etches itself into our consciousness—and, perhaps more importantly, our subconscious. As I write this, it's the height of summer, and when I look out my window I see the deep, lush greens of the sodden vegetation. The morning sun falls on the highest branches of the trees, washing them with fiery orange as new rays peek over the Worcester Range and creep down Cady Hill. Everything's dripping wet—we're having a rainy July. And what do I think of when I see all this July weather outside my window? I think of previous Julys, and how they compare to this one. I remember the wet July we had three years ago, and I remember the hottest, driest July we had, when the canoe kept scraping the bottom of the river bed, and the farmer's fields were scorched brown, and the mice and the deer and the bears moved into the village because there was no water in the mountains. And that's my sub-conscious invoking the cycle within me, and from there, time's only baby step away.

§

When our first foliage season ended and the leaves came off the trees all at once, in wild wind and rain storm (there's that violent change of seasons again), and we were suddenly thrown into stick season, we realized that we'd been innkeepers for one year. And it wasn't the calendar that told us—we didn't look forward to November 20th with the kind of excitement a child looks forward to a birthday. Rather, it was the seasons, the completion of a cycle, and the initiation of another cycle, that sparked our instinct to step back and review our first year as innkeepers. And the first thing we remarked upon wasn't anything that had to do with innkeeping; it was the seasons themselves.

Finding ourselves in stick season wasn't a shock. Discovering that the season we were in actually had a name, and that name had to do with the end of foliage, and was a sub-season of autumn, surprised us. From the time the leaves begin to change colors to the time of the first snows had always been "fall" to me. From that point, to the time the snow melted and the robins came back had always been "winter." From then until the time I could wear shorts every day was "spring." And summer lasted until my birthday, September 23. But now, in northern Vermont, I had to get used to a whole different set of seasons. There was stick season, which goes from the end of foliage until the second weekend in November (about three weeks). Then there's hunting season, which lasts until the first weekend of December. And then there's winter, which lasts until the end of April. That's followed by mud season, a two- to four-week stretch overlapping the end of winter, when all the unpaved roads in Vermont—and Vermont has more of them than anybody else, about 7,000 miles' worth—turn into mud, swallowing up small cars and dogs and Lycra-clad runners. Spring lasts for two weeks, from May 8th to May 22nd, and then summer comes again. That's a lot of seasons to deal with, and I haven't even touched on the variations that can characterize them, like a rainy summer, or a hot spring, or an "up and down" winter with sporadic snows.

Like the arbitrary times set by a company for its fiscal year, our cycle deviates from the calendar, always ending at the conclusion of stick season, during hunting season, around Thanksgiving, which is a good time for us. Thanksgiving provides us with the right forum to reflect, and as our first year as innkeepers concluded, we paused to catch our breath and figure out what we'd learned. We learned how to run, how to just go with the flow and not make waves, and to have a little faith. And it's that last bit—the part about faith—that might be our best lesson from the first year. There's a few different degrees of faith, and I'd like to talk about them with respect to innkeeping.

The first degree of faith is desperation. That's the kind of faith a child has during a nightmare: you hold on, even though you know the end of the nightmare, because you really know you're dreaming, and that you'll just wake up soon, and it will all be over. We had a little bit of that variety of faith, until someone actually came in the door and stayed and ate breakfast with us and left and smiled and said, "Thank you." Even if people don't mean it, "Thank you" is the nicest thing to hear from a guest. Oh, it's not like we were holding each other in the cellar, crying, wanting it to be over, but there's a certain amount of stress involved in any business, especially during start-up. And when someone actually smiles at you and says, "Thank you," you're elated. You're elated because they have the manners to say it, you're elated because they might actually mean it, you're elated because they didn't turn on their heels and walk out the door without staying.

The next degree of faith is exasperation. That's the kind where you see something happening, yet you're powerless to change it. Like the ceiling leaking during the winter. Or the basement flooding when it rains on top of four feet of snow and ice. Or two people showing up with reservations for the same room. That's when you have to step back and believe in the universe, that something will change, sometime in the future, to your advantage. It's the kind of thing that we humans can only let slide off our backs.

And the final degree of faith is called continuation. That's the kind that you want to last and last and last, like a pint of Ben & Jerry's Cherry Garcia. When things go right at the inn, when the breakfast room is full of people babbling in four different languages, and the snow is fresh and falling, or the sun ignites the trees on Cady Hill and the grass is so green it looks contrived, and when all the toilets flush and the pipes don't freeze and the crotchety couple in Room 4 leaves a ten dollar tip, when the hot tub's not boiling over with frothy soap from someone's oft-laundered shorts, when everybody's cozy or exhilarated from a day on the slopes or a day on the trails, and when they all check out early on a Sunday and we have the day to ourselves and we can go out to dinner that night at the Stowehof and watch the sun set and the deer come wandering out—and I'm not going to tell you the rest—but when all that happens, that's when you want innkeeping to last forever, that's when it's the best job in the world.

§

Our first year was filled with both extremes. The big construction projects were satisfying, because they improved the property, which is our major investment, but they don't necessarily put heads in beads, which is how the mortgage is paid. As well as keeping the rain off the guests' heads, the new roof enhanced the look of the inn, so it was an easy sell for us. And the elaborate decking system we had built out back was needed, too, not just because it looks nice, but because there's no other way to get down to the pool that nobody uses (but that everybody likes to look at). Thirty-five steps in all, traversing three decks. But one of the new decks was critical to our plan because that was the deck where the new, outdoor hot tub was going. The story of the old, brown hot tub is well-known already; but the story of the new hot tub is better, and it sort of sums up our first year here.

Whenever Chantal and I shop for a big-ticket item, it turns into a smart contest; we can never come to a decision easily. Things would work so much better if I were a giant dope who spent his days grunting. But I'm not. I have ideas, and she has ideas, and we have to find overlap for those ideas. This results in endless hours of research, because that's the first thing smart people do: they research things. Then you start talking to people. Then you start re-thinking everything. And then you start shopping. At least that's the template we used for our hot tub buying experience. Too bad it didn't help us.

If Florida is a state with a pool in every backyard, then Vermont is a state with a hot tub on every deck. And that means that there are plenty of hot tubs for sale, as people remodel, or get a better hot tub. So we found a great Jacuzzi for sale, just down the road in Duxbury. We went to look at it, and our first thought was, "Oh my God, it's huge!" And it was. It was a large, 6-8 person model, in excellent condition. The guy was selling it because he was remodeling, and he didn't use it that much. We consulted with our deck builder, who assured us that he'd built the deck strong enough to support this big monster, and after a little haggling, we bought it.

With the help of Tommy the Builder and his crew, we trailered it back to our parking lot, covered it, and that's when our problems began. The first thing we learned was that this huge hot tub ran on 220-volt power. We didn't have that kind of power. Our ancient, 100-amp service couldn't take another light bulb added to it, never mind a 1.5 horsepower, two-speed hot tub pump and heater that ran on 220 and drew trillions of amps. A few calls to electricians enlightened us to the cost of updating everything for the hot tub, and since we were officially out of start up money (the last of it was spent on the hot tub), we now owned a hot tub on a trailer in the parking lot, as well as a beautiful, empty, reinforced deck. Enter the first degree of faith.

With nothing but desperation flowing around us, we simply hung on, and boy did we get lucky. It turned out that another innkeeper was in the market for a hot tub, a nice, big one, like we had in our parking lot, and with only a little negotiating, they bought it from us. Halleluja. Suddenly awash in money again, we reset our sights on a hot tub, and now that we were considerably smarter about the whole thing, we knew what we wanted. On thing the big Jacuzzi didn't have was adequate insulation. The previous owners said we could stuff fiberglass insulation into the cavity, but that didn't sound too hot (if you know what I mean, and don't pardon the pun). We envisioned (after we bought it, of course) huge electrical bills trying to keep it hot through the frigid winter. But after we sold it, we discovered that there was a Canadian manufacturer of hot tubs, Beachcomber, who sold completely insulated models. Better yet, we could buy it in Canada for less money, due to the exchange rate, which was still advantageous for Americans back then. Finally, we decided to buy a smaller model, one that comfortably held four adults. With all that going for us, we borrowed a truck, borrowed a trailer, and drove up to Canada, to the nearest Beachcomber dealer.

Buying the hot tub was easy: it came shrink-wrapped, and three burly men loaded it onto our trailer. I lashed it down, and we headed back home. But in all our excitement, we'd forgotten that home had changed, because we did all this two weeks after 9/11. A long line greeted us at the border, and we wondered if we'd be able to get the hot tub into the States. It was made in Canada, and we'd checked the regulations, but all bets were off as the country reeled from the disaster. As we approached the customs stop, one of the agents signaled for assistance. And then he said, "Hey, Eddie (or Al, or Mike, I forget what his name was), come here and look at this!" He pointed to our hot tub on the trailer, smiled, and came over to us. "Hey, nice hot tub, where's the party? Can we come?"

We made it through customs without a problem, thanks to the dominance of human spirit. But when we got home, another problem awaited us: How were we going to get the hot tub onto the back deck? Again, we turned to Tommy the Builder.

Tommy Fletcher was more than just a contractor for us. He was the Shell Answer Man of Stowe. He functioned like a translator, advising us about everything we had questions about during our first year in Stowe. When we needed an electrician, he gave us names we could trust. When we went to the Fourth of July fireworks celebration at Mayo Field, he told us the best place to park (with him and his family, who were enjoying a cookout). And when we needed a way to get the hot tub onto the back deck, he came up with the solution.

At first we thought we might roll it around the corner of the building, then up a ramp and onto the back deck. The hot tub was round, and without any water in it, rolling would be easy. But the building crowds the edge of a steep slope—the same slope that runs down to the back yard and the pool that nobody uses, but that everybody likes to look at, and the path that leads around the north side of the building is narrow. Plus, there's a telephone pole right in the middle of it. But Tommy had a better idea: a crane. For about a hundred and fifty bucks we could have the hot tub boomed over the building and plopped down—gently—onto the back deck. I loved the idea, because it changed my role in the project from grunting and swearing to picture-taking and smiling. It was a no-brainer, and both Chantal's and my brain were happy to be excused from the decision.

There are few sights that can compare with a three thousand dollar hot tub dangling above a bed and breakfast against the backdrop of a blue Vermont September sky. The hot tub looked like an overweight flying saucer wracked with indecision about where to land, as if there were no worthy bodies to bubble its water against in the vicinity. But then, slowly, it was directed downward, gently coming to rest on the deck. Straps were slipped off, and the boom operator drove away, leaving us lighter in the wallet, but very happy.

Throwing the switch on a new hot tub satisfied us with more than just hip Vermont vibes. It allowed us to answer "yes" to two of the most common questions we get when people call to inquire about room availability in the winter: Question 1: "Do you have a hot tub?" Question 2: "Is it outdoors?" Skiers figured out long before we did that the intoxicating mix of hundred-degree water and lightly falling snow and a bottle of wine was the only fitting way to cap off a day of hard skiing. It was a surprising discovery, because we'd always considered ourselves ski bums. But the previous ten years had been spent traveling and living abroad, and having babies, which limited our skiing. Now we lived in Stowe. Now we could properly re-tap the vein of skiing that brought us together in the first place.

§

So without much celebration, we observed our first year as innkeepers. Time, and our perception of it, changed that year. In our reckoning of time, we began to shift away from clocks and calendars, and move toward seasons and sunlight. Our business demanded a kind of stolid, laconic approach. If we had a bad summer, there was nothing we could do about it until next summer. And even then, there's little we can do. Our first year—our first cycle—taught us that external factors far outweigh our actions in determining success. In a destination like northern Vermont, which relies heavily on regional tourism, weather, and potential travelers' perception of the weather, is the first factor influencing traffic. Second is the economy (and, once again, potential travelers' perception of the economy). What we could control was us, our product, our inn. And after our first year as innkeepers, with sporadic business, a recession, and the disaster of 9/11, we figured we wouldn't be controlling much of anything. We knew we could stick it out on paper, in theory. But we were learning that like a marriage, a small business required more than passion and excitement to endure.

Chapter Nine
Division of Labor

I have a guilty conscience. I feel responsible for the problems of the world, and I'm always trying to compensate for that. Sometimes, that feeling comes out in my dreams. One dream I had featured me on a couch in a psychiatrist's office. At first, I thought the psychiatrist was a Dr. Freud type: you know, beard, pipe, Austrian accent (I know that's a corrupted image, but we're talking about my imagination here). But then I realized it was a woman, professionally dressed and hyper-aware of everything I said and did. She wore glasses and looked stern. She never talked, and the only thing I said was, "I like vacuuming." Over and over again, I like vacuuming, I like vacuuming, I like vacuuming. The only explanation for the dream is that it occurred just after a busy summer season, where I vacuumed a lot. Not only that, I bought, sold, reclaimed, and rebuilt vacuums. At one point we had four different vacuums in service, or partially disassembled on my workbench. When it comes to the division of labor at this inn, I'm the vacuum guy.

The sordid tale of vacuums and me goes way back. When I was a child, my grandparents had an ancient Electrolux vacuum, really nothing more than a tin tube that sucked air in one side and blew it out the other. A simple machine, it was effective, and I remember pushing the bar around their kitchen, making dirt disappear. My mother had a high-end canister, a Kenmore from Sears. It was that shade of seventies green found today only among Spanish olives, and the attachment had a motor of its own. The whole thing weighed a ton, and it needed a draft horse to pull it around. We had shag carpets in our house then, and the vacuum would change the visual pattern as you passed over it. I became an artist with that beast.

When Chantal and I moved back to the States, we got a Hoover upright. It was a great vacuum, but it was impossibly loud. The apartment where we lived, in West Medford, Massachusetts, had hardwood floors, and I had to wear hearing protection when I vacuumed. The 12-amp motor was a monster that could pull nails out of floorboards. All you had to do was put it in the middle of the room and turn it on, and everything within a 20-foot radius would be sucked in. We kept that vacuum for thirteen years, vacuuming dirt, dust, toys, pets, and the occasional child who wandered into my path.

My vacuum obsession really took off when we became innkeepers. A friend gave us an Oreck commercial upright, and I was vamped. Besides its intuitive maneuverability, what I liked most about it was the 31-foot cord. I could vacuum the entire inn—including our house—from only four different plugs. When there's a lot of vacuuming to do, stopping to unplug and plug in your appliance is a time robber. Not having to devote thought to outlet placement in an old building is a blessing. Now I could plug it in and fly. But after about a year, the motor conked out, and I had to go back to the big 12-amp beast. One minute of that ear-damaging jet engine sent me running to the Internet. I bought a replacement motor for the Oreck on eBay, and I was amazed at how easy it was to install. In no time I had my freedom—and my hearing—back.

In the interim, though, Chantal had gone out and bought a small, cheap vacuum cleaner. Because you can't own an inn and go even a day without a vacuum cleaner, and because it took me a few days to find the motor and get it shipped here, then install it, we bridged that couple of weeks with this little cleaner. It did a fine job, was bagless and easy to carry around, but it clearly wasn't up to the task of chowing down large trails of mud dragged in by guests on rainy days, nor did it deal that well with dog hair or thick carpets. But it worked well on hardwood floors. So when the Oreck went back on line, we suddenly had three vacuums (And I haven't even mentioned the wet/dry vacuum we kept in the basement). Now I began to flourish as a vacuuming consultant, assigning the right vacuum for the right job. The Oreck still handled the bulk of the inn cleaning. The small plastic vacuum was used in our kitchen and dining room, which had hardwood floors. It was also effective in bathrooms because of its nimble size. The big 12-amp beast had a variety of attachments, including a long hose that made it the choice for cobweb removal and deep corner cleaning. The attachments also made it perfect for cleaning vehicles. This arrangement suited us well, until the Universe decided that we should enter a period of protracted vacuum hell.

One day we were at the Stowe dump, and we saw another Oreck by one of the Dumpsters. I grabbed it, if for nothing else than for parts, and brought it home. Sure enough the first Oreck died inexplicably not long after that. But the dump Oreck worked fine...for a while. Then it, too, ceased to work. Soon I had two Orecks disassembled on my workbench. But no combination of Dr. Frankenstein tinkering gave me a working Oreck. In the meantime, the Universe had decided to throw us a bone, and we found another working vacuum at the dump (over the years, we've equipped ourselves nicely from the Stowe dump, finding everything there except a Porsche 911 SC, and I'm sure the only reason we haven't found one of those is because we haven't hit it on the right day). This one was a Hoover, a standard bagged model, plenty of attachments, not too noisy, nothing special. Most importantly, it worked. We all lived together happily until I decided to interrupt the vacuum space-time continuum again by buying a new vacuum.

What happened was this: we retired the old 12-amp. We left it at the dump, thinking someone would surely find it there and give it a home. After all, we reasoned, we had three other working vacuums. Then we gave away the little yellow plastic one to Chantal's mother. After all, we reasoned, we had (at that point) two Orecks. And then the Hoover from the dump began to act funny. Actually, I had to say the one thing about a vacuum that you never want to say: it didn't suck. And that prompted me to buy a new one. And that could only mean one thing: research. Consumer Reports was consulted, the Internet was sifted through, and other innkeepers were shaken down for their vacuuming secrets. While we would have liked another Oreck, at nearly three hundred dollars a pop, they were a bit pricey. The latest craze in vacuums, the Dyson, was way out of our price range at four hundred plus dollars. I'd been pleased with Hoovers, so I found one that had all the features I wanted: plenty of attachments, bagless, Hepa filter, and a long cord. It was called the EmPower, and it retailed for around one hundred and twenty dollars. But I could do better than that. I found it on Amazon for a lot less, plus I had a gift certificate, so it ended up costing me half of that.

It was a great vacuum right out of the box. It picked up dirt we never knew we had, and the Hepa filter astonished us. I became a whirlwind of vacuuming, happily ridding the inn of cobwebs and dust. And then, about two months after we bought it, the motor burned up, and it, too, fell victim to the worst pronouncement that could be bestowed upon a vacuum: it didn't suck. As of this writing, it's out for warranty service, and I'm hopeful the problem was a glitch, not a flaw. (Author's note: the EmPower is back, and a year after the service, it's running great. In other words, it sucks.)

§

All this talk of vacuuming—and my obsession with it—highlights an important element in the innkeeping business: division of labor. Who-does-what needs to be spelled out right away, so that the innkeepers don't walk around assuming that the other is doing the thing that needs to be done. When that happens, business is affected, directly and immediately. Try checking a guest in and discovering that the bathroom hasn't been cleaned because you thought the other innkeeper was going to do it. But due to the intensely personal nature of innkeeping, division of labor has to be an evolution. Mom & Pop businesses can't survive without a business plan, but that plan has to be humanistic and dynamic and open. It's got to have room for growth, the lateral kind.

When we first moved into our place, my mother-in-law moved in with us. For nearly twenty years she'd lived in Louisiana, where she was a nurse. But after being a widow for two years, she took us up on the offer to move to Vermont. She retired and headed north. Trudy figured prominently in our scheme during the first year. And while we didn't sit down and have a formal discussion about who would do what, things evolved quickly, and here's what the work assignments looked like: I did nothing, Chantal and her mother did everything else. Something had to change.

By the summer of our first year, I'd changed to a part-time schedule, and my role at the inn became clear: maintenance. Depending on your point of view, I was either blessed or cursed to have just enough mechanical talent to keep the old building standing. Much of what I did fell into the "light upkeep" category, things like painting, air conditioner installation and removal, landscaping. But there was another level that demanded a little more skill. That involved things like fixing toilets, wiring outlets, and repairing small engines. I called that level the response level, because usually it involved responding to a situation that didn't exist before someone checked into a room. In other words, when a guest came down and said, "The _____ won't _____," I got the call. I was the one who got to fill in the blanks and tinker with the verb. There's a third level, one that easily surpasses the first two, and I call it the "project level." This is the part of the job that most people hire contractors to do. Things like re-habbing bathrooms fall into this category. So far, I've ripped out and rebuilt three bathrooms. One of the qualifiers that makes something a project-level task is the need for two things: a vacant room and a mixing of skills. Bathroom rehabs require the following skills: planning, plumbing, painting, carpentry, and electrical. Oh, and time. Jobs like that are best saved for one of the shoulder seasons, spring or fall. Don't try it mid-week, between busy weekends. Something disastrous will happen, and you'll lose a booking. Besides, whenever you start working on an old house, you get led on a wild chase.

Every time I go to change a light bulb, I always tell Chantal I love her, and that I love the boys, because I never know when I'm going to be back. Changing a light bulb can set off a chain reaction that tears you from your family for weeks at a time. Things usually began like this: Chantal would say, "There's a dead light bulb in Room 4. Will you replace it?" So I'd go in to change the bulb, only to find the circuit was dead. I checked out the circuit, and discovered that the plug was not functioning. So I grabbed some tools and a new outlet (I have a pile of new outlets on stand-by at my workbench), turned off the breaker, and went to work, thinking, "This is a twenty-minute job, tops." When I pulled out the old outlet, I found the wiring was completely deteriorated, so I followed it back to the nearest junction box, replaced it with new wiring (from the roll of 14/2 I keep on my workbench, next to the outlets), and replaced it all. But when I was replacing the outlet, I noticed a wet spot. Above the outlet, someone had run a water supply pipe for a bathroom sink, and the soft copper had finally decomposed, and was leaking. That's what had helped kill the old outlet in the first place. That had to be dealt with right away—I couldn't have water dripping on an outlet. So I shut off the water, and grabbed my plumbing gear. I also grabbed some copper tubing and copper fittings (which I keep next to the 14/2 wire on my workbench).

The plumbing job wasn't hard, but I had to cut open the wall to do it. After everything was soldered together and leak-tested, I went back to my workbench and grabbed some drywall and trim (which I keep next to the copper fittings). The drywall replaced, I had to finish the job by spackling and painting everything. Like most people, I have about fifty cans of paint filled with hardened pigment on my workbench (next to the drywall, trim, copper fittings, and 14/2 electrical wire). I keep these cans because the People In Charge say I can't just throw them away anymore, that they have to be disposed of on special "hazardous material collection days" at the dump. So I went down to my workbench and began popping open the cans of paint, looking for a can that had some liquid left in it that was close to the color of the wall I'd ripped open to fix the leaky pipe that I discovered when I was replacing the outlet that was broken when I went to change a light bulb.

Finally, I had to clean up, and this meant—hooray!—vacuuming. For me, cleaning up is the most exciting part of the job, because it's my opportunity to make things better than they were. It allows me to focus on an area close-up, in detail, and address any issues—like baseboard grime—that might have escaped our routine inspections. But when I plugged in the vacuum (to the new outlet), nothing happened. No power. No loud vacuum roar. No sucking. I checked the circuit with my tester—it worked. So it was the vacuum. I grabbed one of the backup vacuums and finished the job, then dragged the broken vacuum down to my workbench. Along the way Chantal stopped me and asked, "What are you doing?" I frowned and looked at her. "I'm fixing the vacuum, of course."

She frowned back at me, then said, "When you're done with that there's a dead light bulb in Room 4. Can you replace it?" Or something like that. I honestly don't remember because several days had passed in the interim, and I'd forgotten most of everything else. Except how to fix things, like light bulbs.

§

I've actually got it pretty easy.

Chantal has to deal with just about every other phase of innkeeping. She's the chief financial officer, and the chef. She's also the face of the inn, both to guests and to the greater community of Stowe. As a trustee on the board of the Stowe Area Association, she plays an active role in the direction of Stowe's business community. She also manages the reservations system we use, and she's responsible for the maintenance of the website. When the phone rings, she's the one who answers. When a guest opens the front door in the middle of our dinner, she's the one who gets up from the table. When someone asks me a question, she's the one I turn to. My role is simple: I'm the innkeeper's husband.

But that doesn't mean I'm divorced from all innkeeping duties. When I get home from work, I often help make beds. And then there's the vacuuming. And I spend a fair amount of time taking reservations and checking folks in. But when it comes to the breakfast portion of the program, that's all Chantal. She spends her mornings in the breakfast room, chatting with guests, helping make their experience that much better. And I'm lucky for it, because socially, I'm stunted. I can never figure what to say to someone, unless I've got a script. I'm pleasant and friendly, but I lack the gene that allows me to probe through the possibilities of a conversation. I've done a little experiment before, and it goes like this:

On a busy morning, when Chantal is out in the breakfast room chatting away, I encouraged her to sit down for a minute and eat some breakfast. While she ate, I walked out to fill up my coffee, and tried to say hello to the guests. People looked up at me, and I greeted them with a big smile and said, "Good morning," and waved. I even said, "How are you folks doing?" to one table. But they grunted and stuck their noses back into their food. Could this be the same group of people who were just laughing loudly with Chantal? And when I was able to engage someone from another table, it lasted only a few lines.

Them: "Is there any more jam?"

Me: "Sure. Chantal made that jam. It's got raspberries and red currants in it."

Them: "Where did she go? I wanted to ask her about that."

Me: "I'll go get her."

Even when guests want to talk about my book (my other book, *Name the Boy*, the short story collection), the conversation is usually stunted.

Them: "You wrote a book."

Me: "Yes, I did."

(Silence; then crickets; then a lonely train whistle in the distance.)

Them: "Is Chantal coming back?"

Me: "I'll go get her."

I know what you're thinking: I'm the one who's missing the possibilities of the conversation. And you're right. Instead of saying something like, "Yes, I did," I should come back with, "Do you read many short stories?" Or, "Have you ever read any short stories in the *New Yorker*? They suck compared to mine." Or "I'm offering a discount to guests who buy a copy of the book." There are a million different conversational venues open to me, but the present for me is like a fog. Only after time has passed, and the fog has lifted, do I get to see things clearly. And by then memory has laced things with its own seasonings; I've fictionalized things.

I've got a theory about this dynamic between Chantal and me, and how it distributes itself across our roles as innkeepers: What would it be like if I were more gregarious, more of a goodfella? What would that be like? The two of us, standing out in the breakfast room, talking away? On one hand, that would present a nice picture, the unified front, the couple who are both the same person. But that's not Chantal and me. She doesn't want to be me, and I don't want to be her. In fact, we crave the differences in each other. We're like opposite, but interlocking, pieces of a puzzle. Yin and yang. The net effect is more dramatic, and more true. It's who we are, so it's honest. That honesty is one of the things we can offer as innkeepers. Because we're not here just to take your money, because we're not here just to make a mortgage payment, and because we're not here so that we can say, "We're innkeepers in Vermont," we can give you the only thing we have: ourselves.

Chapter Ten
Gnashing of Teeth

If there's one notion potential innkeepers should divorce themselves from, it's that innkeeping is anything but a business. It isn't a hobby, a diversion, or a lifestyle choice. It's a small business—the worst kind—and it must be run that way. No matter how deep the pockets of the owner, small businesses are subject to the same variety of dizzying rules and regulations as other entities. While these may vary from locale to locale, one thing is immutable: as soon as you open up, everybody lines up with their hands out. We certainly weren't blind when we entered this venture. We understood that there would be lots of new things to learn about running a business in Vermont. But we figured that since we were coming from Massachusetts, the land of regulation, things would be easier. One of the first rule issues that caught our attention was the pool.

I've made it abundantly clear that I'm not a pool guy. There's no love lost between chlorinated water and me. So when we came up to look at the Auberge before we bought it, I grunted at the pool. Set far out in the backyard, the remarkable thing about this pool wasn't its enormity (40,000 gallons), but its lack of enclosure. There was no fence around it. We mentioned this to the realtor showing us the property. "This is Vermont," Bob said. "We don't need fences." He was right. A quick drive around town revealed that almost no other pools were fenced in. In Stowe, more people have man-made ponds than pools, and none of the ponds were fenced in. Even the insurance agent assured us that a fence wasn't needed. That assurance lasted about four years. Then we got the notice from the insurance agency that the pool needed to be enclosed. What a surprise.

Agency backfilling became sort of a theme with us, and it's that way with many business people. A ripe example of this happened a few years into our tenure here. Chantal suddenly noticed that more money than we'd budgeted was being withdrawn each month to pay our mortgage (we were on the automatic withdrawal system). She called the bank and discovered that forced flood insurance had been placed on our property, without our consent or knowledge. Incredibly, this was legal. Somewhere in the bank, someone included our property among those lying in the flood plain of the Little River, which flows behind the inn, at the edge of the property. That triggered the forced placement on the list, with the surcharge automatically added to our mortgage to the tune of nearly $10,000 a year. Chantal, budget maven, lost her mind. Her eyes bulged and she frothed at the mouth. Someone was going to die, or at least be provided with the opportunity to die.

The bank was useless. They shrugged their shoulders and said it wasn't their call, that FEMA—the Federal Emergency Management Agency—regulated that, and that they were just following the rules. After much gnashing of teeth and wringing of hands and kicking of asses, we found someone at the town hall to help us, who said we had to get the property surveyed and prove that we weren't in the flood plain. We knew we weren't, but we still had to get the property surveyed, submit everything in triplicate, and hope the brainless ghouls running this scam figured things out in our favor. It was a huge and stressful and unnecessary exercise, and it demonstrated again that in a small business, you can't be passive. You have to be ready to face all challengers, from telephone marketers to government curs. But as bad as that episode was, it paled in comparison to what we went through with the Vermont Department of Labor and Industry. And that all started with a kitchen.

§

The kitchen we inherited when we bought the Auberge was ghastly and outdated. It was separated from the dining room by a huge bar that was five feet off the ground, nearly impossible to see over. The sink was ancient and of a variety of chipped porcelain that collectors now pay huge sums for. The cabinets extended to the ceiling, and were painted a dusty cream color that was certainly a result of lead in the paint breaking down. Some shelves had been tacked onto a wall, with louvered doors that offered the mice just enough privacy, while still allowing light to filter in so that they could see what they were doing. Only the refrigerator and dishwasher were new-ish and worth keeping.

As soon as we absorbed the initial financial shock of moving up here and starting a business, we faced the kitchen. Chantal knew what she wanted, and she knew where to get it: Ikea. So we gutted the kitchen and drove up to the nearest Ikea in Montreal and came back with a snappy new kitchen. Ikea kitchens are European in style, and that means they're systematic. Everything's assembled and hung and mounted and when finished, it's solid and functional and lovely to look at. The best part was that I could do it all myself—all of it, that is, except the electrical rewiring.

This old house came with an ancient 100-amp electrical system. The electrical panel was the old fuse type, and it was managed by replacing fuses whenever one burned out. It was one of those things we knew we'd have to address at some point, and that point came with the renovation of the kitchen. I have enough skill and knowledge of electricity to do the basic things, like rewiring a plug, or moving a fixture, but this job was bigger than that. Several new circuits needed to be created, and that would push the old 100-amp system over the edge; we needed to upgrade to 200 amps. So we started calling electricians. And none of them started calling us back. Because of the high-end housing boom in Stowe, it's nearly impossible to get a tradesman like a plumber or an electrician to do an annoying job like upgrading an old building to 200 amps. Why bother? It's dirty and a pain in the ass. When there's tons of new construction jobs worth huge money, it doesn't make sense to beat your brains out on a job that doesn't pay that much.

When we did find a couple of electricians to give us estimates, they were all over the place, and so were their recommendations. Some said we needed a major overhaul that would cost us close to ten grand; others said we wouldn't need an overhaul, but that it would still cost us ten grand. This led to more gnashing of teeth and wringing of hands. Finally we figured it out: the more people we asked, the more opinions we'd get. We'd mistakenly thought that there was a rulebook to be followed, and that the only variation in the prices we'd get would be based on availability and labor. Now we knew that wasn't true. Each electrician would do what he wanted, the way he envisioned it. None seemed particularly expert in code as it related specifically to our building and our project. So we cherry picked. We told the electrician we liked what we wanted and he did it. Our service was upgraded to 200 beautiful amps, and when he was finished, the electrician called the electrical inspector in for the okay. The electrical inspector came in, gave the job the thumbs up, and then noticed that our fire alarm system hadn't been inspected in ages. He pulled out his cell phone and called the Department of Labor and Industry inspector, and we were officially fucked.

After living a few years in Vermont, we were surprised to discover that there was an electrical inspector. It made sense that there would be one, of course, but everything else had been run so folksy that we were lulled into complacency. We were doubly shocked at his diligence. And we were knocked out by the arrival of the inspector for the Department of Labor and Industry. His name was Paul Cerutti, and he arrived within an hour of being called, as if this was an emergency. He went through the inn with a magnifying glass and an evidence bag. When he finished with us, we thought we were finished as innkeepers.

The first thing Mr. Cerutti said was, "It's been sixteen years since this place was inspected. All the code has changed since then." And that's how he said it: mechanically, factually. We thought we'd left that sort of regulation-speak behind us. The next thing he said was, "I'm going to need more time for this," and he scheduled an appointment to come back and do a complete inspection.

We didn't panic, but that was mostly out of ignorance. We'd been dealing with the health inspector for a couple of years, and we knew what to expect from him. But this guy was a mystery. We figured he wanted to look at the fire alarm system. We felt good about the other systems. The electrical had just been inspected, and our heating system was serviced yearly by the folks at Bourne's, who were good about letting us know if anything needed some work or updating.

This guy Cerutti was like a cat, and I suppose he had to be. He was expressionless as he methodically picked through our building. Ironically, he spent less time looking at the fire alarm system than anything else. "You're fire alarm is out of date with its inspection. You need to contact someone to inspect it," he intoned. As a sidebar he told us that all the smoke detectors in our rooms needed to be hard-wired with a battery backup. He also noted that many of the bathrooms didn't have ground fault circuit interrupter plugs, and they would need to be updated. As he breezed through the breakfast room, he noticed an extension cord and informed us that we couldn't run anything, not even a toaster, from that. Then he got to the windows.

In Room 1, there was a large bay window, fixed, that was in violation. The reasoning was that in a fire or emergency where the door was blocked, a person wouldn't be able to escape. Cerutti didn't buy my argument that they could just throw a chair through the window to get out. The window would have to be replaced. A similar situation unfolded in Room 6. The windows there were too high off the floor, due to the height of the lower roof outside. There was no way we could ever lower them, so we were told that we'd have to install some kind of ladder to reach them. And then, they, too, would have to be replaced, because they were too small to fit through. It was hard to argue with this. Whenever I have to get out on the roof, I go through Room 6, and my slender hips barely make it through. The double-hung windows in that room were tiny. I didn't even bother with my breaking-the-window argument.

But the most frightening code we seemed to violate had to do with the hallway. The board of health licensed us for occupancy up to thirty people. This was ridiculous because we could only sleep twenty-two. But Cerutti explained that since the last inspection, the rules had been rewritten, and now anyplace that could accommodate more than sixteen people would be classified as a hotel, and subject to the more stringent safety requirement of those larger establishments. Specifically, that meant 20-minute fire walls in the hallway and steel fire doors. We would have to get our official occupancy reduced to sixteen in order to avoid a financially fatal and uglifying construction project for the back hallway.

Other add-ons that the good inspector tossed on us included safety railings on the stairs leading down from our new back deck, and handrails in the stairs. He also told us that we couldn't store anything in the basements that were home to the heating systems—or at least there needed to be a four-foot buffer around the furnace. By the time he finished with us we were reeling, wondering if our innkeeping experience had just been cut short. But mostly we were trying to comprehend how this could have happened. When we bought this place, our diligence—such as our questions about the pool needing a fence—was met with a smile and wave. Chantal was fuming. She specifically asked the attorney we hired to handle the transaction to research any and all code updates that needed to be addressed so that we could more accurately negotiate a price with the sellers.

Cerutti had left us with a laundry list of items to work on. He told us to follow up with him, in writing, when the violations had been addressed. While I started on that, Chantal turned her attention to our attorney. How could this have happened? When she was brushed off, she got tough, and said she'd be taking action in small claims court. But what got us attention was when she said she'd be contacting the Vermont chapter of the Bar Association. The lawyer settled with us the day before we were scheduled to appear in court and cut us a check for our troubles.

Meanwhile, we had to deal with the fire alarm. For that we had to hire a local electrician. One glance at the panel and he declared the system out of date, and failed. We also discovered that the whole system was faulty. All of the sensors that had been installed in the guest rooms were dummies—that is, they were connected to nothing, and had there ever been a fire, the fire alarm would have done nothing. But since we were reducing our official occupancy to sixteen, we wouldn't need the fire alarm system; hardwired smoke detectors would be enough. We still needed to get the alarm panel removed, and until then it was graced with a "fail" sticker.

Strangely enough, it's not the Department of Labor and Industry that controls our occupancy. That falls to the Board of Health. And when we contacted them about our occupancy, they shrugged us off and said we couldn't be licensed for sixteen because they only issued under thirty and over thirty permits. Trying to explain to them what we'd just gone through with Labor and Industry was futile. The right hand didn't know—or care—what the left butt-cheek was doing.

Eventually we got to almost everything on the list. The smoke detectors were hard-wired into the rooms. I replaced all the plugs in the bathrooms with GFCI units. I added a safety rail along the stairs leading from the deck. I sheet-rocked the stairs leading to the basement with adequate fire stop. I cleared the areas around the furnaces and boilers. I added a fire door to the basement. And biggest of all, we replaced the windows in Rooms 6 and 1. Room 1 got a huge sliding window that a baby grand piano could fit through in case of a fire. Now, whenever people call to book a room, I always ask, "How fat is your ass?" If they say, "Very fat," I put them in Room 1, so that they won't be rendered during a fire. Room 6 got new windows: two, barn-door style that swing open, so that guests can crawl out onto the metal roof, then slip off and plunge to their deaths during a fire.

§

My morbid humor shouldn't be interpreted as a sign of hubris regarding all these inconvenient rules and regulations.

I'm grateful for the information, and a lot of it makes sense. But Vermont has only one inspector for the whole state, and how he decides to spend his days is a mystery to me. Obviously, other inspectors will call him up if they see something that needs his immediate attention. But if this is so important to public safety, perhaps more resources should be devoted to it. I'm also expressing frustration at the way things were presented to us, from the realtor, to the former owners, to the lawyer we used for buying the place. The whole thing was a train wreck in slow motion, and we were left responsible. Adding to that aggravation was the knowledge that we tried to get this done during the transaction—we knew what would happen. And like the time when I asked the former owner where the town dump was, and he told me "on Dump Road," that sort of folksy bullshit doesn't pay the bills, and it doesn't excuse you from legal imperatives. Like I tell my kids about school, there's a time for fooling around, and there's a time for learning in the classroom, and the two never, ever overlap. It was an unpleasant lesson for us to learn—even though we knew it already—and it was no fun for our lawyer, who got his pocket lightened.

Most of all, the whole episode illustrated how the notion of innkeeping differed from its reality. Whether you're doing this as a hobby, or a lifestyle, or a small business to make money, you're never exempt from the pressures of society and government. It was almost enough to make us close our doors; it may yet.

Shawn Kerivan

<u>Chapter Eleven</u>
Shtick

Picture this: You're driving up Route 100, and you enter Stowe. To your left is a huge, open field, conserved through a land trust. Views of Mt. Mansfield rise beyond it. Continuing along, you pass a dairy farm, then a building used as the home of a local advertising firm. Across the street, tall pines stretch into the blue summer sky. The Lower Village bustles with two gas stations and convenience stores, a large hotel, and a string of cute looking shops. Once in the village, one of the largest and oldest hotels looms over the intersection of Routes 100 and 108. Up and down the Mountain Road resorts and hotels dominate the scenery, interspersed with restaurants. Finally you reach the base of

Mt. Mansfield, with its imposing luxury hotel hulking at the foot of Spruce Peak.

And that's about it.

What's missing?

The small inns. The B&Bs that give the town a richness of character are all gone, driven out by various things: economic forces, apathy, and my imagination. For this is not the reality of Stowe, but only a possibility. There are perhaps a couple of dozen small inns—places that would qualify as B&Bs the way most people imagine them—in and around Stowe. There used to be more. Since we've been innkeepers, we've seen about a half dozen just go away, close their doors, sell, and cease to exist as a small inn. Three Bears at the Fountain, one of the most successful places, closed its doors when the owners moved to Florida. The Moscow Tea Room B&B recently closed. The Stowe Bound Lodge, across the street from us, has become commercial space. The Butternut Inn burned to the ground. The Scandinavia Inn, Anderson's Lodge, The Seibeness, the Woodchip Inn, Miguel's Stowe Away, the Spruce Pond Lodge, the Burgundy Rose, Foxfire Inn and Restaurant, the Winding Brook Lodge—all gone, none replaced. Even Larry Heyer's Ski Inn, one of the originals, has vanished. Is this a harbinger, or a natural part of growth and contraction found in the business world? Small innkeepers may comprise only a part of Stowe's character, but without us,

Stowe isn't Stowe, and without Stowe, we're not the inn-keepers we've become. It's a relationship that transcends symbolism.

Stowe is a complicated, rich place of contrasts in perfection. You only have to drive the length of Route 100 to see the difference between Stowe and everywhere else. And that's not to say that Stowe is better; just different, because along the road will be other idyllic settings, as well as tired, run-down ghosts. The road offers all things Vermont. But pulling into the village, there's a vitality and energy that at first blush may look managed. Upon closer inspection, though, there's nothing managed about anything, except a desire to be a part of something original.

Like all mountain villages, Stowe sprung up at the confluence of two rivers—streams, in this case. The Little River and its West Branch meander through a flood plain, and Stowe is perched just a few feet above them. While Stowe has been many things throughout the years, it is mostly what it is now: a vacation destination, sprinkled with farming. Recently, Stowe's population has shifted decidedly away from strictly a business venture. More and more people are settling here, discovering that they can work and play in the same spot. Each morning the road is full of people commuting into Burlington. And as those people come here to live, huge networks of support systems have sprung up or expanded to serve them. Public works like schools, police, and fire departments are larger than ever. Road crews work furiously through the winter to keep the snows at bay. Supermarkets loom in Waterbury and Morrisville, on each side of Stowe, along with smaller markets in the village, to feed them all. And many businesses completely unrelated to skiing or tourism call this place home, from advertising agencies to architects to investment firms.

The net result from all this non-tourism industry and settlement is an increase in property values. And what's bad about that? After all, the Auberge has doubled in value from what we paid for it, at least. Taxes go up, but that's to be expected. The real villain in this scenario is the inability of the community to sustain small businesses—not only our B&B, but other places, like Col d'Lizard, which made their own line of clothing, or Lackey's General Store. When property values rise beyond a certain point, the businesses they house cannot sustain them. Here are some examples.

Turnover in the innkeeping business is natural. The industry average for duration is 5 to 7 years. That's about the time frame needed to get a place running successfully, then burn out. Think of it as the seven-year itch. But if a small innkeeper decides to sell, soaring property values can be the enemy. In our case, the value of our property has doubled. No one can come in and sustain the business at that level and afford the mortgage. This scenario assumes that the next owner would have roughly the same profile as us, and as small innkeepers go, we're fairly typical. So anyone occupying our situation the way we did when we bought the Auberge would be excluded from getting into innkeeping. That means that somebody with enough money to run it as a hobby could buy it and keep it going. But people with that kind of money aren't generally in the market for an old-fashioned roadside inn. Their tastes run more toward higher-end places. Or they'll just build a new one themselves. So that means that the only thing people like us can do is sell the property commercially. This is what happened to the Stowe Bound Lodge. With Three Bears at the Fountain, the property was sold as a private residence, and judging by the wide variety of license plates out front from weekend to weekend, the place is used mostly as a rental.

The net result is a reduction of mom-and-pop places. If that's true, then let's look at what Stowe will be without them. And before I go on, it's important to remember that this is just an exercise. I'm not suggesting that a proliferation of dinky little inns, stores, and shops is the solution to the inherent problems of this new business model. I'm more interested in the transition and projection of this.

If Stowe has one thing in its favor, it's the prohibition of chain stores. By keeping mega-retailers and franchise fast food out, Stowe has been able to preserve its charm, at least on the outside. Assuming that rule stays in place, and assuming that only people with enough money to afford the rising property values continuing moving in, a picture of Stowe's future emerges. It's a place with lots of high-end boutiques run by people who don't need to meet the bottom line because they have enough money to do this as a hobby. Their clientele will be their neighbors—people with the same income level, so their products will all be at the extreme high end of price and functionality. While the village will look lovely on the outside, it will be dead on the inside, because there will be no middle class, just the very rich and the very poor who drive forty-five minutes in from the hinterlands to work for them. Stowe will approach a level of artificiality unseen before, because not only will the town be home to this unbalanced model, but it will cater only to people with enough money to come here. Gone will be the middle-class and upper middle-class travelers. In their place will be people who can afford to pay four or five hundred dollars a night for a room and breakfast, then another hundred dollars a night for dinner, and several hundred dollars for skiing. Stowe could become a ten-grand weekend: a lovely, untouchable place.

Or course, everything's cyclical. I alluded before to the natural expansion and contraction of things economic. And a little of my view is based on bemoaning the fact that we got in at the end of the last bust, and we're now in the boom. We should be thrilled. But our goals aren't just to be filthy rich, otherwise we'd be there by now. When we became innkeepers, we were looking for something different, an alternative lifestyle. We wanted to be in a place that drew us outdoors, and we wanted to share that with other people. It's the business model of our inn.

Our relationship with the town has been easy, and that's mostly due to our philosophy. We haven't embarked on major development, and we're not big enough to matter. We've just come in, taken up innkeeping, and integrated ourselves into both the business community and the residential community. Having kids helps with the latter, and being a small business helps with the former. The Stowe Area Association is the engine that drives the economy here in town, and it was easy for us to become members and take advantage of their marketing efforts. It's all added up to exactly what we wanted out of our innkeeping experience, if not exactly how we envisioned it.

I think our original notion of innkeeping involved us having a place not unlike what the Auberge has turned into, but set in a wilder spot. Maybe up on the side of a mountain, ten miles from a village. At least that's what I wanted. I'm a loner, and I crave solitude. The problem with the scenario I just described is that it doesn't work when all the other factors orbiting around us are plugged in. If you're going to be out in the middle of nowhere, guests are going to be looking for something more than just solitude. There needs to be a reason to drive far out of the way, something more than just stuffed French toast. In other words, you have to have a shtick, and shticks cost money. Let me explain.

Imagine that you're a young couple—or an old couple. One of you is a car mechanic, the other an insurance salesman. That's all you've done. You're happy, you've raised a family—or maybe you're still raising a family. But you've got a dream about being innkeepers. You want to buy this gorgeous farm and turn it into a B&B, so you save, and you do it. But besides just being a nice place to stay, why are folks going to come to you? It's a ten-mile drive into the village, where there's only one restaurant, and that's more like a diner. What are folks going to eat at night? Are you going to feed them dinner, too? What are they going to do after they check in? Stare at the million-dollar view of the Green Mountains? Swing in your hammock? Then what? How much can you charge for a product like that?

While there is a market for that experience, it's not very big, and it takes a lot of time an effort (Internet marketing) to find customers and drive them to you, especially for the first few years. And if you've spent all your money buying the place and fixing it up, you won't be able to ride out the first few years of monetary misery. And since you live way out on a farm, it's hard to support yourself as a car mechanic or an insurance salesman. But, if you have a shtick, you can partially overcome some of this. Perhaps you create an English garden and you serve afternoon tea. That's something to hang your business hat on, because it can be marketed separately from your inn. People will go out of their way for that. Or maybe your car mechanic business has allowed you to accumulate classic cars over the years, which you display in your barn. Plus, you fix classic cars, and that's something people will come out of their way for. That's your shtick. It's your way of raising your hand in a noisy classroom and saying, "Pick me, pick me!"

Stowe is our shtick. Well, maybe not really. It's our meta-shtick, the big blanket we crawl under at night. But it's pretty crowded under there, and we still need something to differentiate ourselves from this place crowded with luxury. And what we've decided to do is offer people an experience they can't easily find in Stowe anymore: the small, affordable roadside inn with an emphasis on simplicity. We offer the classic European B&B experience: unpretentious and genuine. (Hmmm, is it pretentious to say you're unpretentious?) And as long as we continue to occupy that niche—that affordable price point in an increasingly unaffordable market—and offer the individuality that can't be picked out of an interior decorating catalogue, we'll continue doing what we're doing. It's our shtick.

Chapter Twelve
Character and Caricature

One day, I found myself standing out in front of the inn with an ax.

Our woodpile is to the left of the front door, and when we need wood, I usually go out with my ax and split a few quarters into manageable sticks for the Franklin stove. The funny thing about splitting wood for me is that I do it in a very public place, so that everyone driving by can see the ax-wielding innkeeper. Great for business. One afternoon, as a group of young people from Boston was arriving, I was out chopping wood. I didn't realize it until later, but I looked the part all too well: plaid shirt, wool pants, boots, work gloves, greasy ball cap, and an ax resting on my shoulder. The only things out of place were my glasses and the soft look to my pale, Irish face. I paused and watched them pilot their vehicle into the driveway. This usually isn't a tough assignment. Our driveway is the wide strip of hard pack that separates the inn from the road. Finding it involves pointing the car at the parking area and stopping before you crash into the building. But these folks seemed to have their own ideas about parking.

As they tried to take a left turn into the parking lot, the car lurched forward and stopped several times. The driver couldn't decide if the breaks in oncoming traffic—some of which lasted several minutes—were enough for him guide his car across the ten feet of open pavement to our lot. Inside the car I could see gesticulating, semaphores, and American Sign Language. Wanting to help, I stepped out so they could see me, and waved my ax at them, pointing it toward the empty lot. It wasn't until later that I realized a car full of college students from the city might not interpret a man waving an ax at them as a welcoming gesture. My thrashing only added to the cacophony of distractions for the driver. Finally he managed to get his foot on the gas pedal long enough to push the car across the street, and they skidded to a stop. That's when I got into the act.

Unfamiliar with the climate, they stumbled out of the car in short sleeves, then stood around shivering. I walked over to them, and instead of being myself, I became the caricature of an innkeeper.

"Howdy, folks," I said falsely, affecting the nasally twang of northern Vermont. "Welcome to Stowe. If you've got any wood that needs splittin', you've come to the right spot!" I twirled my ax for punctuation, and everybody took a step backwards.

This act continued later, as I hunched in front of the stove and prepared the fire. A couple of the guests came out to watch—or to urge me on, because they were cold. I stuffed newspaper in the bottom, topped it with dry twigs and scrap wood, and plopped a big quarter section over everything. Then I stepped back and obviously admired my work.

"Are you going to light it?" asked one of the guests.

"Well," I said, pausing and pushing my ball cap back up on my head for effect, "I'm not going to frame it." Haw.

The next day, some guests remarked that they'd seen some people hiking in the woods wearing blaze orange. (It was November, hunting season.) They asked if it was dangerous to be in the woods with hunters.

"As long as you don't grow antlers you'll be fine!"

Oh, God.

And that's when it finally hit me. That was the moment I heard myself trying to be someone—something—I wasn't. I wasn't a local—I wasn't born here. But I was no longer a flatlander. So what was I? In my heart I felt like I was in "belonging purgatory," an empty place devoid of identity. I wanted to blame my exterior for this feeling, but it really came from within me. It was a manifestation of my own identity crisis. I had devolved into a caricature of myself.

§

After about three years as innkeepers, something happened: we began to get repeat business. First there was the couple who came every year during foliage. They're from Florida, and it's their annual escape to the North. Room 6, every time. Then there's Andy and Mike, brothers from Connecticut, a couple of charming ski bums, one masquerading as a fourth grade teacher, the other pretending to go to graduate school, both of them lifelong ski junkies. And there's Rob, a naval aviator, former F-14 Tomcat pilot, who stays with us whenever he comes up to visit his kids. Mary comes up every year for the garden festival in June. And there's a whole cadre of regulars who come for Antique and Classic Car Show weekend: Ernest and Betty (Room 1), the Withams (Room 4), and Mary Dapkins and her husband. Many of our regulars have become more than customers. They've become friends, extended family members. Like Trevor.

After coming up here to go to Johnson State College, Trevor, like so many other people, became hooked on

Vermont. For many years he owned a condo near the base of the mountain, and he came to ski and play and relax there with his family. But the condo fell victim to divorce lawyers, and when Trevor found himself looking for a new base in Stowe, he found us. Now, when he comes with his boys, one of them uses the piano in our dining room to practice his lessons. And when I graduated from Goddard, Trevor came to the party, and as a gift brought me a framed map of Mt. Mansfield from the 1940s that had hung in his condo for years.

Relationships like that take years to forge. And obviously, they don't happen with everyone who comes through the door. But a rotation of regulars signals a turning point for innkeepers.

How to get those regulars isn't as easy as just surviving for a few years. There has to be a reason for folks to return to your inn, and it's not the breakfast. No single element will win the innkeeper repeat business, because innkeeping is like dating. What appeals to one traveler repulses another. While the rich, young couple will drive past a funky little place like ours on the way to a $400 a night palace, a couple from the Netherlands will seek us out, fly across the Atlantic to get here, and when they arrive be shocked that luxury inns actually exist. It's a matter of finding your crowd, that vein of humanity that lights up when they see your website, or drive past your inn. And what excites them, what draws them in the beginning, what brings them back season after season isn't you, and it isn't your fluffy pillows, and it isn't the view, or the fireplace—it's all that, together, and it's called your innkeeping shtick.

Don't think of shtick as a gimmick; think of it as a seam that you occupy in the dense fabric of life, love, and work. Shtick isn't the design on your sign, though a sign that reflects who you are rather than whom you want to attract can become part of your character. And character isn't caricature, and it isn't the way you fold the bedspread under the pillows, but if that's a part of who you really are, then that goes into creating your identity. What's important to remember is that it can't be created, only recognized. And once you recognize who you are as an innkeeper, your guests will recognize you, too, and then they'll come back, again and again.

When we bought the Auberge, we were lucky to be very close to our shtick already. We understood who we were, and that we'd match up well with a small roadside inn. Our family was our priority, not spending or making vast sums of money. We came here to raise a family and ski and enjoy all that Vermont had to offer. (Notice in that last sentence there's nothing about innkeeping.) Innkeeping would fit into our lives, not the other way around. Guests soon tapped into that vibe, and that's when we began to be successful. But don't think we didn't have our share of missteps—our own growing pains.

I was especially susceptible to this in the beginning, as I struggled to see who I was in the picture. There was the onus to keep my job with FedEx, which I viewed as cutting me out of the innkeeping picture. Then there was the role I played around the inn: head of maintenance. They were my two primary functions in life, and I didn't recognize myself in either of them. It wasn't until I began writing again—first for the Stowe Reporter, then for my master's program at Goddard College—that I began to feel like I was in my own skin.

§

I don't think we can ever really avoid being who we exactly are. And if we try too hard, it shows, on the outside as well as the inside. For me, that meant losing that nasally northern Vermont twang. I decided that I was just going to take this innkeeping thing as it comes, and if that meant chopping wood, I'd do that; if it meant emptying the hot tub in the middle of winter, stripping down to my shorts, and climbing in to clean it, I'd do that. Whatever it took, and I'd just be myself about it. I'd write about it. My shtick would be me, which is exactly what it was anyway.

I like to think of shtick in bigger terms. I like to think of things as star systems. Like our earth, revolving around our star (the sun), and our sun, revolving around a bigger system (the Milky Way Galaxy), and that system, moving around a bigger force. Our life at the Auberge became a little star system, spinning through the seasons of the year, concerned with its own orbit, but aware of the bigger things we revolved around. Other people and businesses in Stowe were other star systems in our galaxy. But the Big Kahuna, the object with the greatest pull of gravity, the thing that bends the fabric of space all around it, causing us to stay nice and close to it, is the Mountain. Capital M.

Chapter Thirteen
Who's Your Daddy?

Every innkeeper needs at least two things: shtick and a sugar daddy. We've already explored shtick as your own particular odor, the thing that makes you jump up and down in a crowd and say, "Look at me!" But what's a sugar daddy? A dictionary friend of mine defines a sugar daddy is "a rich,

older man who lavishes gifts on a young woman in return for her company or sexual favors." That may sound a little harsh, but it's a fact of life: in business, in the tourist industry, and in innkeeping. The small business-person is the ingénue of the economy, and the sugar daddy is the one uncontrollable element that becomes the raison d'etre for the industry. In Stowe, the sugar daddy is Mt. Mansfield.

Let's take that definition of sugar daddy and transcribe it so that it makes a little more sense, and doesn't sound as hard or as cynical as it really is. First let's try translating it into generic business terms: "An established customer need that supports a variety of associative enterprises." There, that sounds nice and clean, doesn't it? But what the hell does it mean? At its heart, it means that people want something, and when they find it, they assign it the role of sugar daddy. As long as the sugar daddy continues to exist, and as long as the people continue to want it, other things are able to survive around it—the sugar daddy, that is.

Now let's look at Stowe. The sugar daddy is the mountain. People want to come to the mountain. (It's the oldest of all human desires; the first thing our ancestors said when they climbed down out of the trees was, "Let's go to the mountains for the weekend." The second things they said was, "Let's go to the beach," but that's another book.) If the sugar daddy definition is translated into Stowe terms, it sounds like this: As long as the mountain continues to exist, and as long as people desire a visit to the mountain, we'll have a robust industry in Stowe based largely upon that phenomenon, supporting a variety of businesses, like lodging, restaurants, and women's shoe stores selling $400 stilettos.

If you look carefully at that last sentence, you'll see that business in Stowe, like every other business ever conceived in the history of mankind, is based on the three essential needs for survival: food, shelter, and expensive shoes—er, I mean clothing. And in every business microclimate, people are going to be looking for some version of that formula to compliment the sugar daddy. Before deteriorating into a broader discussion of the humanistic approach to economics, it's worth noting that the Stowe model is a basic one, with a clearly defined sugar daddy. It might be more difficult to clearly identify the sugar daddy of, say, New York City. But it's there.

Every once in a while in Stowe, a conflict burbles to the surface. It pits the business community against the residential community. And by residential community, I mean people who have moved here over the past 20 years or so, who are wealthy enough to own a million dollar home with only one income earner, and who usually have children. The issue that comes to the surface usually does so after a busy period in Stowe, such as after our run of peak foliage, or after the Antique and Classic Car Show weekend in August, or after President's Day in February. During those busy times, the town swells with tourists who choke the roads, restaurants, and shops. Checkout lines at the Shaw's supermarkets are obscenely long. The intersection of routes 100 and 108—which constitute Stowe's downtown—are clogged, filled with drivers from New Jersey and Massachusetts who think stop signs are a suggestion, not a law. Huge tour buses constipate the narrow village streets, stopping incomprehensibly to discharge elderly travelers onto the sidewalks.

If you're a local resident who enjoys going to the bank, bumping into a neighbor or friend, standing in front of the town hall and chatting, or sitting in front of the Stowe Mercantile with a cup of coffee and the paper, times like those described above are harrowing. Life is disrupted. Vermonters who are habitually late become chronically late, or just don't show up at all. The kids are late getting home on the bus (that is, the few who take the bus are late; for the vast majority, who are dropped off and picked up at school by their mothers, getting near the elementary school is impossible, which leads to more kvetching). In short, unless the pantry is well-stocked and you're prepared to hunker down, Stowe becomes a challenge.

The tone of the conflict varies, but in general terms it's an argument by residential citizens bemoaning Stowe's focus on its business community at the expense of its quality of life. But when asked why they're here, why they came to Stowe, everyone, business owners and gentleman farmers alike, all give variations of the same answer: the Mountain. Stowe's beauty is directly attributable to the Mountain. And my response to people is always the same: if you take the Mountain away, then Stowe is just another Vermont village. Pretty, yes, but indistinguishable from scores of other crossroads. And without the Mountain, there are no Mountain views. And without Mountain views, there are no astronomically priced pieces of real estate. There's no prestige in bragging that you live in the Ski Capital of the East, there aren't dozens of world-class restaurants, and the von Trapps probably wouldn't have settled here.

The funny thing about the conflict is that it always recedes. That's because it's not a disease that needs to be cured; rather, it's an intestinal malady that flares up when we eat too much.

It would be nice to think that Chantal and I were cold and calculating enough to have analyzed the situation in Stowe, compared it against other locations, run simulations, and then entered into our business. A lot of other innkeepers do just that. The phenomenon of creating luxury B&Bs is such a high-stakes game, with so much money involved, that nothing short of a battle plan and a willingness to run into a machine-gun nest is needed for survival. Chantal and I weren't looking for anything like that. We wanted to ski and live, and there were only three places in New England we'd even considered: Sugarloaf and Sunday River in Maine; and Stowe. As mountains go, Sugarloaf and Stowe share a lot of similarities. But the reason we ended up here was because of the place we found for sale. That's pretty much the extent of our planning: Find ski area, buy inn.

What allowed us to be so cavalier in our planning was the sugar daddy effect. We knew that no matter where we ended up—Kingfield, Maine, Steamboat Springs, Colorado, Courchevel, France, or Stowe, Vermont—we would have what my father calls a "money pump." A mountain with ski trails and consistent snowfall, surrounded by a deciduous forest, and crisscrossed with hiking trails and roads to access them, is a money pump. There are few, if any, of these mountains left undiscovered and unexploited. Even Jay Peak, sitting on the Canadian border an hour north of us, is sprouting condos, golf courses, and women's shoe stores the way a teenager sprouts zits before the prom.

What makes Stowe special among other areas is its history—with respect to both Vermont and to skiing. Stowe began life thousands of years ago when the glaciers that formed much of New England's craggy landscape receded. Stowe was one of the deep valleys left behind, a channel between Mt. Mansfield and her handmaids on one side, and the Worcester Range on the other. A small river drained the land into the Winooski, which itself flowed into the lake that Samuel de Champlain would "discover" in 1609. The land that is now called Stowe, with adjacent Mt. Mansfield, remained devoid of white men until 1793, when Oliver Luce skidded his way into town on a sled. Another settler, Captain Clement Moody, followed him the next day. And the path from Waterbury to Stowe—now called Route 100—has been busily shuffling people into town ever since. Recognizing that Stowe was situated in between the valleys of the Lamoille and Winooski Rivers—and understanding the flow of commercial traffic between those two waterways—one of the first things Mr. Luce did was hang a sign outside his cabin on the north end of town. The sign said, "Vacancy," or something to that effect. Stowe's first settler was no dummy; he was also Stowe's first innkeeper.[4]

Nothing much really happened in Stowe for the next hundred years or so. I'm joking, of course. Lots happened. Lumbering dominated the economy as forests were laid bare, potash was exported, farming arose on newly opened land, and with the coming of the train in the mid-19th century, real tourism arrived. People came to Stowe for the summer air, then stayed for the glorious turning of the leaves (which now grew on the deciduous trees that had repopulated the barren landscape). By the early part of the 20th century, Stowe was well-known as a two-season resort. With the arrival of some Scandinavian families around 1913, Stowe began its relentless journey toward the title of Ski Capital of the East.

By 1921 Stowe boasted a Winter Carnival, and that represented man's total dominance over his environment: just a century earlier, people were trying not to die in the cold and snow; now they were making money off it. At first, ski jumping was all the rage. But two things changed that in the 1930s: the first was The Great Depression; the second was Sepp Ruschp. As part of the New Deal, the Civilian Conservation Corps was created to put idle men to work. In Stowe, that work took the form of cutting trails on Mt. Mansfield that would be used for the new sport of downhill skiing. Soon after that, Sepp Ruschp arrived from Austria and established Stowe's first ski school, setting the tone for Stowe's future.

After World War II, the good times rolled. As the national economy expanded and people found themselves with leisure time available, places like Stowe experienced growth in the tourist industry. Lodges and restaurants popped up along the two main roads to service the visitors. Sometime in the 1950s, in what was now Stowe's Lower Village, an old brick farmhouse began offering accommodations. It called itself the Brick and El. In the 1960s a family bought it and changed its name to the Lower Village Inn. In 1986 a retired engineer and his wife bought it, and called it the Bittersweet Inn, after the vine that grew wild on the trellis out front. And in 2000 a young family from Braintree, Massachusetts—via France, Montreal, and

Green Harbor—bought it, and called it the Auberge de Stowe.

From all this history comes the Mountain as sugar daddy, and our intersection with it. It's interesting to note that Stowe wasn't established as a resort at the foot of Mt. Mansfield. It was a good old-fashioned land grab—or grant, as it was called back then. And it's still going on to this day. Stowe Mountain Resort—the Mountain Company—has embarked on a radical makeover, changing the face and function of the Mountain in a way that hasn't happened since Charlie Lord pioneered the original trail cutting with the Civilian Conservation Corps in the 1930s.

If there is one certainty in all this, it's that the sugar daddy isn't going to change, and it isn't going away. Mt. Mansfield will be there, at least for the foreseeable millennia. It's not a volcano, so it won't erupt itself into extinction, a la Mt. St. Helens. Erosion will get it someday, but none of us will be around to see that. The Mountain will continue to dominate Stowe. Men and women will come and go, drawn to it. That won't change. What will change is the base camp, and the Sherpas, and the way the rice is boiled.

What will change is everything else.

<u>Chapter Fourteen</u>
The Writer

In his book *The Beatles*, Bob Spitz documents the greatest band from their humble start to their endless influence on our society and culture. One of the most fascinating things in the book is the discovery that neither Paul McCartney nor John Lennon ever learned to read music. The music they made was the music they heard in their heads. What astonished me was how Paul would walk around for days, months, or years with a tune in his head, never bothering to write it down. Most famously was "Yesterday," which he fooled around with on the piano for years before it became the most recorded song of all time. Another was "When I'm Sixty-Four," from Sgt. Pepper's Lonely Hearts Club

Band. The tune was written when McCartney was 14, and they'd been trotting it out on stage since their Hamburg days, but he'd never written it down.

When I read this I nearly dropped the book. It was exactly the way I wrote. I'm flooded with ideas constantly, and I discovered years ago that if I write them all down, they look like crap. But if I ignore them, only the pesky ones stay with me. That's good because those persistent ideas are the ones with truth, energy, life. And that's been my career as a writer: my muse pursuing me while I flee before it. I'm not saying that I'm the creative equal of Lennon and McCartney.   And yet...

§

By now you may be wondering, "Just who is writing this book, and how does he know so much about the Kerivans and the Auberge de Stowe?" If you haven't noticed the author's last name, now's the time to check it out. Go ahead, look at the cover. See? It's me. I'm the author, and the innkeeper—the innkeeper's husband. But I'm the one who does all the writing around here.

This writing thing has been dogging me for a while. It all started with baseball. During the summer of 1975, when I was ten, the Boston Red Sox were tearing their way through the American League. They were loaded with legendary talent, like rookies Jim Rice and Fred Lynn; Hall of Famers, like Carl Yastrzemski and Carlton Fisk; and great characters, like Bill Lee and Luis Tiant. Those Sox won 95 games en route to an American League Pennant before losing the most famous World Series in history to the Cincinnati Reds. Like any true Red Sox fan, I wasn't satisfied. Especially with the baseball writing.

I had nothing to do that summer. My mother worked all day, leaving my brother and me home alone. (It wasn't that bad; we lived in a nice neighborhood, and all the other parents kept an eye on us.) Every morning the Boston Globe arrived, and I went to the sports page to check the box scores from the game the night before. What I saw in those box scores never seemed to match up to the stories written about the game. So I started writing my own stories, divining from those cryptic boxes what might have transpired with my heroes, according to my own imagination. Day after day I banged out stories on an old Royal typewriter, filling reams of onion-skin paper. At the same time, I was reading. Not age-appropriate works for a fifth grader, but adult novels. I tore through John Jakes' series chronicling the rise of an American family. James Michener was nothing to me. I devoured it all. The three R's of my education were readin', (w)ritin', and Red Sox.

Fifteen years later, I found myself trying to invent myself as a writer again. This time I was in a little 2-room apartment in Mulhouse, France. I'd moved there with Chantal, when she took a job as a regional marketing director for Sodexho, a giant food service company. Since I had no talents save reading, writing, and following the Red Sox, I spent my days conjugating French verbs and hunting down baguettes. By the time we left France, nearly three years later, I'd turned myself into a writer and a fairly proficient speaker of French. I began publishing my stories in small literary journals, which seemed best-suited for my character-driven approach to fiction. But those little rags didn't pay much, and life demands action for the paterfamilias, and as sons were born and houses were bought, then traded up for Vermont inns, the onus on me to work cut seriously into my wish to write. Finally, in 2004, Chantal and I decided that I should pursue a master's degree in writing, not only for the sake and advancement of my craft, but as a way to get into teaching, which would spring me from my enslavement to FedEx.

The story of this inn and my writing are so closely entwined as to be nearly indistinguishable. And like any relationship, this can be good, and this can be bad. This little triangle—me, my writing, and the inn—has no shortage of intrigues, and the three of us have shaped each other in unexpected ways.

From the outside, it looks like a perfect match: writer and innkeeper. After all, what could be more perfect for a writer: sipping the fresh coffee he's brewed for his guests while he hunkers down before his old Royal typewriter—er, I mean, Apple iBook G4. And what could be more perfect for an innkeeper: meeting interesting travelers, building a roaring fire in the Franklin stove, settling down with a toasty glass of Scotch to reflect on the day's inspirations. And in more ways than that, it is the perfect match. The problem is that the same things that influence the writing are the same things that influence the innkeeping, and those influences aren't always positive. Of course, I'm talking about the elephant in the room, the crazy uncle nobody wants to acknowledge: the mortgage. It's the common denominator that cancels out everything else.

Think of life for the writer without a mortgage: days would be filled with mugs of coffee with my morning writing; long walks with the dog as ideas percolated; time to spend with my family hiking, biking, and skiing. And think of life for the innkeeper without a mortgage: days would be filled with mugs of coffee with my morning writing; long walks with the dog as ideas percolated; time to spend with my family hiking, biking, and skiing...

Wrong. Toilets would still back up. Manuscripts would still be rejected. And I'd still get phone calls from whatever school the boys were attending: "Mr. Kerivan, I'd like to speak to you about...." The problem with a mortgage isn't that it's a financial commitment; it's that it reflects life so accurately. There are no days off in life. There are no montages scored with beautiful transition music. Every day is a new job, a new responsibility. Innkeeping and writing just happen to be the things I do on top of the mortgage. After we became innkeepers, it didn't take long for my writing and my innkeeping to encroach on each other. And FedEx was to blame.

As good a fit for FedEx as I was when we lived in Braintree, I was a poor fit for the job up in Vermont. I knew it the instant I walked into the station in Williston, and I was never able to synchronize myself to operations up here. Things got worse when I was injured, and even worse when I came back from my injury. After six months, I was ready to quit. But there was that mortgage thing, plus the fact that during our first six months as innkeepers we didn't break any monetary records. But I tried to find a new job anyway, and as I said earlier, one of the places I tried was the Stowe Reporter, our local weekly newspaper. While I didn't get the job they advertised (I'm not a journalist anyway), I did get noticed by the editor, and he invited me to pitch him an idea for a regular column, and that idea turned into an 18-month run called "InnSights."

InnSights started on June 7, 2001 with a story about mornings at the inn. An editor's note explained the new column this way:

Shawn Kerivan and his wife, Chantal, embarked on a great adventure last year. They bought an inn in Stowe. In the first few months, the hot tub drained mysteriously into the basement, merry-making customers passed out in the front hall, and when Kerivan uncovered the pool, his first thought was to call the high school biology class for a field trip. When he's not fixing leaky roofs and shooing squirrels from the basement, Shawn actually makes a living driving a Fedex (sic) delivery truck. And like most Fedex (sic) driver-innkeepers, he's a writer too (sic) with ambitions as a novelist. So he proposed a column on the adventures of innkeeping, and what better place than Stowe for such a column? Thus Inn Sights was borne. Look for it bi-monthly.5

Writing that first column, then seeing it in print, was about the worse thing that could have happened to me as a writer. It fanned the smoldering coal within me, the ember of my desire to create. Writers view any kind of success with suspicion. Failure is much easier to deal with, plus it has the benefit of providing more material to write about. But now I was writing again, in a public forum, and people liked it. People began to recognize me as "the writer." This only encouraged me to write more, which I did. Plus, the Reporter paid me twenty dollars per column, and money to a writer is like guns to a revolutionary.

While things plodded along at FedEx, Inn Sights—or InnSights, as it became—gave me a goal to work for with my writing, which was something I'd never experienced. Before that, my writing had been purely abstract; that is, everything I'd written had been done for artistic reasons. I'd never posed a question to myself, then tried to answer it. This wasn't an assignment from the newspaper; this was me assigning myself a task, marketing it, then following through. It was a completely new feeling for me. But I loved it. I looked forward to the columns the way a parent looks forward to seeing their children come home from school. It drove me, and it fed my other writing.

There seemed to be no end of topics to write about: crazy guests, crazy family members, systemic failures, attacks by the weather, injuries, famines, plagues, floods, recycling, caricatures, a high school reunion, shoveling snow, chopping down trees, fixing lawnmowers, trying to decide whether or not to add televisions to the rooms, laying carpet, remodeling kitchens, remodeling bathrooms, remodeling hallways, laundry, hot tubs, pools, and Zen. It was a good time, a growing time, for my writing. The need to produce something fresh ever other week kept me focused. The need to relate it all to innkeeping kept me creative.

In the background, however, lurking like the mortgage, was FedEx. Things had changed for me there, as I went from full-time to part-time. Most days I could be home by noon, thanks to an ungodly start time of 5:30 a.m. This meant that I had to get up at 4:30, shovel some food into my mouth, and drive the 35 minutes into work, where I slung boxes for an hour, then scooted over to the airport to work on the ramp crew that handled the 727 that flew in each morning with all the station's freight. Then it was back to the station in time to jump into a truck and deliver packages for the balance of the morning. It was busy, but it left me the afternoons to work around the inn, and that was an important thing.

The effect of InnSights was to make my writing more important, and more legitimate. But then, after nearly a year and a half, the column ended. The editor of the paper came over one day and explained to me that he had never been a fan of the column (it was Biddle Duke, the publisher, who'd been the one to sign me up for the job), and further, they couldn't pay me any more. That editor must have known that I had a strict rule: no money, no writing. I don't write for free, especially for profit-based businesses like newspapers. Too many writers desperately give their talents away to money-making enterprises, and I'd decided long ago that I'd rather suffer than do that. So I thanked the editor for the opportunity to write for the paper, and that was the end of InnSights.

Now I was faced with another problem. I'd advanced myself as a writer, but I didn't know where I was heading. I'd been noodling around with more short stories, and I was a hundred pages into a novel I hated, but I found myself adrift, again. I had a responsibility to the two jobs I already had—FedEx and the Auberge. But neither of them were me, and worse, I began to view them as feeding off each other. To keep the Auberge going, we needed the FedEx job, and FedEx needed me to be an innkeeper in order to stay with the job. So we opened up the discussion about me going back to school.

At first, this meant finishing my undergraduate degree. I had spent four years at the University of Maine at Orono in the mid-eighties, and I was still ten credits shy of a diploma. I didn't finish because I goofed off my freshman year, then ran out of money as a senior; it was always my intent to work a little more, then earn those last few credits. But after I'd moved back home, to Massachusetts, I discovered that the University of Maine wouldn't accept any transfer credits from the schools I wanted to attend. So I said the hell with it, and got on with my life. First I thought I'd build a career in the wholesale fish industry. I'd been working for a friend in the business for several years, and there were plenty of opportunities there. But then a chance to work with my father as a carpenter came along, and I took that. I planned on getting my contractor's license and following that path. But the economy crashed in the late 80's, and I found myself out of work. That's when I ended up as a ski instructor, met Chantal, and we moved to France. Still no undergraduate degree.

As my writing developed in France, I began to question the need for going back to school. I was teaching myself more about my craft, and I was reading more literature than I ever had done in a classroom setting. I realized my education was incomplete in many ways, but I was also living in France, then Montreal, and then I owned a B&B in Vermont, and I just couldn't see what difference a math class, a science class, and an elective were going to make in my life. Of course it's not about the difference they might make in my life; it's about the difference they might make in someone else's estimation of me, should I seek that estimation out. And as I slowly and stubbornly learned, we all seek that estimation out sometime. And so, around the winter of 2003, we began to talk about school again.

At first, we naturally talked about finishing the credits needed for my undergraduate degree. A lot had changed in the years since I had written off the University of Maine's inflexibility. Now there were online classes, and other schools were willing to accept transfer credits in order to enroll you in their program. But then a friend of ours said something that stopped me. She suggested I contact the graduate school at the University of Vermont. Sometimes, she said, they accept students into their graduate program even if they don't have an undergraduate degree. And since I was a writer with a substantial body of work—with only a ten-credit gap in my undergraduate degree—I might be accepted. So I checked out UVM. But before I got too far in the process, another school captured my attention: Goddard College.

I'd been reading about graduate writing programs and the MFA—master of fine arts—that they offered. There seemed to be an endless supply of these schools, but two things made Goddard jump out at me. First was the low-residency program, which Goddard had pioneered as a way to offer non-traditional students the opportunity to continue their learning. The low-residency model works like this: twice a year, students gather at the school's campus. There they attend classes and workshops, meet with advisors, connect with other students, and formulate a study plan, which they will follow throughout the upcoming semester. Through regular submissions of work to their advisors after the residency closes, students demonstrate progression through the planned learning cycle. Evaluation by the advisor based on how the student achieved the goals agreed upon by both at the beginning of the semester wraps up the process. This enables two things: first, the student can keep their regular life. They don't have to stop what they're doing two or three times a week and drive to the local college to attend a class. It also allows them to be full-time students, earning their degree in two years. And they have more choice in programs, because they only have to travel twice a year to attend the residencies.

The second thing that attracted me to Goddard was their philosophy. In a creative writing program, this is no small thing, no ad hoc Latin motto meant to attract attention to the creator of the motto and not the program. Goddard is steeped in the philosophy of the needs of the student. Throughout the program, students are encouraged at every level to discover what their course of study means to them, not just what it means to academia. The way this fits in with a writer is simple: in order to succeed, a writer needs to be aware of who they are. Goddard brings writers to that place and allows them to fill the space of their potential. Goddard also allows students to bring along their work in the real world and apply it as credit, either toward a degree program, or, in my case, toward consideration as an applicant to the creative writing program. All the writing I'd done over the years, all the self-teaching I'd done, all the publishing added up to something after all: I was accepted into Goddard's MFA in

Creative Writing program. My first residency would be at the end of June, 2004.

When I look back on those two years, it's a good thing I didn't realize exactly what I was doing. I don't mean from a writing or from a learning point of view; I mean from a work point of view. I was truly ignorant of the amount of time graduate school would consume, never mind the fact that in order to graduate, I'd have to produce a book-length piece of fiction deemed publishable by the Goddard faculty. My days never ended.

I had to be up by 4:30 a.m. to get to work at FedEx. That lasted until lunchtime, sometimes later. I was always trying to get out of work early, and FedEx always wanted me to cover other shifts and stay later. Once at home, I faced a fresh set of chores. The Auberge demanded work, including regular maintenance and upkeep, as well as project-level work, like painting the building, or re-plumbing a bathroom. There were family commitments, as well, like Cub Scouts for the boys. By some unlucky twist of fate, I became the Scoutmaster, a job I had neither the time nor the talent for. But it was important to the boys, so I found a way to make it happen.

I found myself in the same situation with Stowe Youth Baseball, which consumed most of May and June. Then, in the evenings, the absolute worst time of day for me as a writer, I'd have to tackle my schoolwork. That meant reading, writing, and reflecting. I'd go as long as I could, usually ten p.m., then fall asleep for six hours or so. And the sleep was important; I considered it part of my job. Not only was I driving a truck around the public roads all morning, I was also at the FedEx ramp at Burlington International Airport. Mistakes could cost lives, or millions in damage, and the consequences could be severe.

Being at Goddard did more than open the door to my learning. It gave me some critical balance that I'd been missing, something to counter the aggressive, full-speed ahead life I'd been leading as an innkeeper, husband, employee. Goddard demanded reflection, and for me, that meant confronting the genesis of my writing. It meant asking myself what I truly wanted to write about.

Chapter Fifteen
The Book, The Inn, and The Coffee

It was a pretty good party. Coming during the extended Fourth of July weekend, the party was for me, to celebrate my graduation from Goddard. We had a full compliment of guests at the Auberge, but none of them minded the crowd of newly minted writers and their attendant families. Half of them were from Goddard anyway, either students or their families, staying with us for a few days. So it got big.

But one guest and party-goer stood out—I'll call her "Rita." I remembered speaking to her some months earlier, when she called to book the room. She asked what kind of things would be going on in Stowe over the Fourth of July, and when I told her that I'd be graduating from Goddard College with an MFA in Creative Writing, she exclaimed "Mazel tov!" Without saying too much about herself, Rita seemed interested in hearing all about my Goddard experience, and about my writing. And about the prospects of a party, she said, "I'll be there."

When I met Rita, I knew instantly she was a force to be reckoned with, much like the forces of the Goddard faculty: she was an artist. And the kind of art Rita produced came from her vocal chords. Her personality matched her voice: rich, complex, smooth, layered. Rita was charming, and when she spoke to you, she made you feel like you were the only person on Earth at that moment. Rita was an actress—a voice actress. That explained the mastery of words, and the mastery of the tone, inflection, and volume used to deliver them. She was always ready with her words, employing a variety of accents and characters to fit the moment. And she loved a good party.

My party turned out to be pretty good. Guest from the inn mingled with friends from Stowe. And every time I saw Rita, she shouted "Mazel tov!" Soon other people picked up on this, and began returning her Mazel tovs with Mazel tovs of their own. You could find Rita by following the sound of the Mazel tovs. She managed to turn a party for an Irish Catholic kid into another kind of mitzvah altogether.

Toward the end of the party, as folks began to drift out, Rita grabbed me and sat me down. "Dahling," she said in a voice reminiscent of Ann Bancroft, "you simply must try this." She pulled a flask from her pocket and poured some clear liquid into a glass. "Smell," she said. Then, whispering, "Drink." I knew it was gin immediately, but it was different from any I'd had before. This was floral, with a huge nose that I could have enjoyed by just sniffing. But it was far smoother than expected. And smoothness, in alcohol, is always a dangerous thing. This danger was named Old Raj.

I'm pretty sure Rita left me out in the breakfast room sometime before the sun went down, but when smoothness is involved, you can never be sure. For the rest of her stay, Rita vamped us, and as she checked out a few days later, she turned at the door, and one last time said, "Mazel tov!"

§

It wouldn't be right to go any further without talking about how this book came to be, because this is not the book I wrote while at Goddard. It's the book I wanted to write while at Goddard, but a tall, unflinching man with a Chicago accent and a laser approach to the craft had different ideas. Richard Panek, who would become my advisor and most trusted inspiration, gave a class on nonfiction writing during my first residency at Goddard. I was confident—cocky, even—and I trotted out a manuscript called "InnSights: The Story of the Little Inn that Could." It was a sweet and funny and smart beginning to what I thought would be an account of our lives as innkeepers, and it was full of the kind of writing that I'd been stumbling over for years. For proof, please see the title.

In that first class with Richard—called A Master Class in Creative Nonficiton—he went through all the submissions, mine among them, and offered critiques. From those critiques he created lessons about writing that we could apply to our own projects. All the submissions had been copied and distributed to the class ahead of time, and several of the women in the class came to me and said how much they liked my story. Then it was Richard's turn. "It's too cute," he said. "It's too sticky and sweet. It sounds idealistic. Where's the conflict? Where's the adversity you had to overcome? Where are all the good stories about how things went wrong? That's what the reader wants to see. Not this..." He looked at the manuscript in his hands and I took a step back as I sensed the bile rising in his throat.

In my mind, I'd blown up on the launch pad. I'd been so sure, so confident of my writing, my skills, that I never saw anything like this coming. Tweaking? Polishing? Sure.

But this? In effect, Richard said don't even bother. Start over. Or do something different.

"Don't worry," said a woman who came to be a great friend and great teacher. "I thought it was wonderful."

Though there may have been parts that were wonderful, Richard was right. It crushed me to admit it, but I wasn't even close with that manuscript. I went back to my portfolio and made a tough decision, one that would affect everything from my earning potential to the way people would view me, as both a person and a writer. I decided to work on fiction while at Goddard, and put aside the story of the inn. The more I thought about it, the more it made sense. We were only three years into innkeeping then, still experiencing change, still unsure of our future. And the skills I'd acquire through the creation of a fiction manuscript would only buoy all phases of my writing.

I plunged into the dark world of my fiction and began writing short stories about the things I knew best: fishing, fathers, and sons. During my first year at Goddard, Richard was there with me, guiding my efforts in a way that allowed me to learn from my own writing. In effect, I was teaching myself, but learning how to teach myself. It's the kind of through-the-looking-glass approach that Goddard has perfected.

The work that emerged from this two-year intensive treatment was a short story collection called Name the

Boy. It was a dark, accusatory look at the life I'd come from as a boy in Green Harbor, Massachusetts. Populated with alcoholism and dysfunction, Name the Boy was deeply satisfying to write. In it I was able to explore the limits of my writing, my technique, and my imagination. I discovered the joy of revision, and I embraced rewriting as a primary function of the writing process. I knew that writing a collection of short stories would never be commercially appealing, but it was the right thing for me to do then.

Fiction also allows a story to be told without the fidelity to accuracy that memoir demands. Instead, the fidelity remains with the truth, because the maddening pursuit of facts can be distracting and ultimately unapproachable. While the accuracy of the truth in fiction is undeniable—or should be—the accuracy of fact is nearly inconsequential—or should be. In other words, people should not be able to point to a work of fiction and say, "That's me." They should be able to point to a work of fiction and say, "That's true." And that's the difference between writing fiction and writing a memoir, which I didn't want to do. Writing a memoir would have required reliance on information that was vague at best, unverifiable at worse. Conversations would have to be re-imagined, and facts would be general. In the end, most memoir butts up too close to fiction for my writing sensibilities, which is why I shy away from that form. But writing fiction allows the author to look back at the consequences of things, not just the things. From there it becomes a matter of shaping and molding to fit the idea of the art in the writer's mind.

But wait! I know what you're thinking! You're thinking that this is a memoir. This is an account of me as an innkeeper—as an innkeeper's husband, at any rate. And, well, it is. So why am I writing a memoir, after just decrying its limitations? I think it's because there's been a level of maturity attained not only in my writing (thanks mostly to Goddard and Name the Boy), but also in our experience as innkeepers. As I sit here writing this, we're in our eighth year. More importantly, we're still learning, still experiencing new and different things. Everything's fresh, and can be rendered more truthfully than if I looked back through the distortion of time, when it would surely become more fictional, or at least more selective. What that means is that it's time to tell this story. Like wine in a bottle, this story has reached a level of drinkablility that will last only a certain amount of time. And now is that time. Cheers.

§

I do not, under any circumstances, recommend writing a book in order to obtain an advanced degree while maintaining a schedule as a FedEx courier and second in command at a B&B. It's exhausting, surreal, and when I look back on it now, I can't believe I did it. I'm still tired.

My days—already documented as deliriously long—would go on forever. And I always felt like I was cheating the inn, like I was doing my work there. And as seen earlier, work at the inn could be anything from bed-making to plumbing to light construction. The hell of this schedule wasn't that it lasted eighteen hours a day, ending only when I collapsed into bed sometime between ten and eleven at night. No, the hell of it for me was that I'm a morning writer, always have been. I do my best work at the crack of dawn, with diminishing returns thereafter. For me to begin the real work of my writing sometime after six in the evening was anathema to everything that made me me—at least from a writing standpoint.

But somehow I managed it. I imagined myself on a professional hockey team as right-winger with limited talents (that image wasn't much of a stretch: I grew up a hockey player, except I was a defenseman with limited talents). My job, I told myself, was to go into the corners and get pounded by the opposing defense and dig the puck out. Grind it out. Work hard, sweat, exhaust yourself, and get no glory, score no hat tricks, take lots of Advil. It was that workman mentality that allowed me to plow through a part of the day where I was at my lowest. That, and coffee.

Coffee played more than the typical role in this whole endeavor. Halfway through my MFA program, my work situation at FedEx changed dramatically. FedEx has always been the primary shipper for Green Mountain Coffee Roasters (GMCR) in Vermont, and they've always had two to three people working on a permanent basis at Green Mountain's Waterbury production and distribution facility. About the time my second semester was wrapping up, a position opened up at GMCR's new location, and I snapped it up. I was officially retired as a courier. The new job had several advantages, as I saw it. First, it was fifteen minutes from my house, a leisurely drive down Route 100 to Waterbury. Second, my start and finish times would be fixed: 0600 to 1100. No more fluctuating, no more waiting for the plane to arrive, no more fighting with management over hours. Third, by virtue of the fact that we were seamless with GMCR's operation, there were two paid fifteen-minute breaks each morning, and I was able to spend that time reading and notetaking. I soon became known as "the FedEx guy with the book." And fourth, there was coffee, to which I'm hopelessly and happily addicted. I was entitled to all the coffee I could drink at work, a dizzying variety of roasts and flavors, most of which I explored the first day on the job, and thereafter with moderation.

The job did have one major drawback: lifting boxes. And since this was the main function there—loading boxes into a trailer by hand—it was fairly significant. Loading boxes that weighed anywhere from a pound to fifty pounds for five hours at a time took its toll, and each morning I was drenched with sweat and aching. But when eleven o'clock rolled around, I rolled out. A huge stress had been removed from my life, and while another, more physical stress had been added, I felt the trade-off was worth it.

Everyone who earns a master's degree has to overcome adversity. Everyone has their own private hell. I had mine. But my eyes were focused on the end, and I was able to incorporate that knowledge into acceptance, to make it part of the fabric of me, and reach my goal. In June, 2006, I received an MFA in Creative Writing from Goddard College. And then I received an offer from a small press in Maine to publish my thesis.

<u>Chapter Sixteen</u>
Scrambled Eggs

I would never call my decision to have my creative thesis published a mistake. Nor would I call it a nightmare. Or a disaster. Or a disappointment. No, I wouldn't call the experience an abortion, a train wreck, a useless exercise in futility, or a hideous aberration of nature. I wouldn't even go so far as to call it the biggest regret of my life. But it didn't release any endorphins.

Well, that's not true. Having the publisher accept my manuscript was a thrill. And opening the box and seeing it filled with my books was an even bigger thrill. Seeing people react to the physical presence of my book staggered me: their eyes widened, their heads nodded; they had clearly never met an author before. And on a visit to Washington, D.C., my brother-in-law, Charles, feted me, toasting me repeatedly with my favorite single malt, a 16-year old bottle of Lagavulin. That was tops.

The rest of the experience ranged from aggravating to FUBAR.

The unstated goal of every writer is publication. Whether that means writing a letter to the editor, or writing the Great American Novel, seeing your words in print—ink, on a physical page—is the Holy Grail. It was certainly mine, and it was something I'd had minor success with throughout the years. But the various forms of publication I achieved satisfied neither the artistic nor the monetary goals I'd set for myself. By the time I entered graduate school, my net income from all my published works, spanning nearly fifteen years of writing, was probably under one thousand dollars. But income should never be the goal of the artist, or so we're told. This theory was driven home recently while I was listening to an interview with the actress Tilda Swinton on National Public Radio. She said, "The idea of art making profit, and the idea of making art in order that it make profit and not making art if it looks like it's not going to make profit is anathema to me."[6] Oh, to be so high-minded on NPR. What a luxury.

If we artists aren't supposed to make a profit, what the hell are we supposed to do? I realize that Ms. Swinton was speaking within the context of commercial film distribution in the United States, and that she was bemoaning the lowest common denominator mentality that leads to blockbusters like Pirates of the Caribbean: At World's End. But I prefer to try and find the artistic merit in any film I watch. Even though many movies are insipid, they do entertain, and that's the point. And besides, making a movie—at any level—costs a lot of money. Whether you're a kid with your parent's digital camera, or Martin Scorsese, producing a film takes dough. On the other hand, you can buy a box of pencils and a stack of legal pads from Staples and write a book for under ten bucks.

I never had delusions about Name the Boy. After all, it's a short story collection, and when's the last time one of those clawed its way up the best-seller charts? But I was goal-oriented, and first up was getting my MFA. Then I set my sights on getting my creative thesis published. Inspiration for that came from John Irving. Irving has always been one of my biggest influences, and it started with The World According to Garp. I read the book when I was thirteen, and it changed my life. First, its irreverence not only astounded me, but it resonated with me. Here was a voice that reflected the sounds of my own soul. Here was black humor, immense tragedy, and a rollicking story. I didn't know that Garp was a Bildungsroman, a coming of age story (actually, it's a Kuntslerroman, a coming of age story about an artist, but I digress); I only knew that in T.S. Garp I'd found someone I could finally relate to.

But Irving had done something else extraordinary, something I wanted to accomplish, too, and that was the publication of his creative thesis, Setting Free the Bears. Only in retrospect has Bears become important, because it reveals many of the techniques that would later make Irving famous, things like a reliance on biographical details as plot elements, bizarre sexual and violent situations, and bears. It was probably bears that connected me instantly to Irving. I understood immediately what he saw in bears, and that's a caricature of humanity. I've always harbored a preternatural obsession with bears, and the first story I wrote at Goddard (which appears as the final story in Name the Boy), called "The Natural History of the Bear," shows inspiration from Irving, and fidelity to something essential about me.

Of course, while all this high-minded intellectual masturbation was going on, there was still an inn to run, a job to tend, and kids to raise. I wish I could look back and describe exactly what I did then, but like so many things in life that present a challenge, you overcome by immersing yourself in the moment. I do remember invoking the image of a hockey player grinding it out in the corners, absorbing hard hits, hanging my head in exhaustion. And I remember my mother having heart surgery right in the middle of it all.

When someone in your family gets sick, everything stops inside your head. Outside your head, everything keeps going. When I got the call that my mother had been rushed to the hospital and diagnosed with a failing heart valve, I could hear the tires screeching on the pavement. At that point, my whole life became a series of compartments, and I became their administrator. I quickly arranged my schedule so that I could be with her, then set off for Boston in one of the worst snowstorms I've ever driven through. Somewhere near the New Hampshire/ Massachusetts border it stopped snowing, and I relaxed my grip on the steering wheel. By the time I found some off-street parking near Brigham and Women's hospital, it was around 8 p.m.

My mother was stable, and scheduled for surgery the next morning. My brother and I stayed with her a few hours, then I left for my father's, only to return the next morning. Delays pushed her surgery back to the late afternoon, and she wasn't wheeled into recovery until late that night. The surgery was successful, and she faced a long recovery. She's now in great shape, healthy and happy and relaxed, living in Vermont, about an hour south of me.

The whole experience reminded me that we can really do nothing about life. It comes and goes. If anything, it reinforced the themes in my writing, especially how selfishness and material desire robs the spirit from us. I'd been writing about the smallness inside people, how they became consumed with their own pettiness and addictions. Seeing my mother go through her own looking glass, and seeing her emerge on the other side spiritually awakened told me I was on the right path with my work. It was only by delving into the darkest side of my characters' nature that I could reveal the hope that waited at the end of the stories.

My mother's illness also spoke to our approach as innkeepers. After the dust had settled, Chantal and I didn't have to look around and question our values. We weren't immersed in a meaningless pursuit of materialism. Our whole approach to innkeeping had been contrary to the conventional wisdom; we sought to give people a different experience from the one everyone else offered. Chasing the luxury dollar in innkeeping was cliché, and it definitely was not us. What Chantal and I did realize was that we could live with ourselves if something bad happened. We could say that we'd tried to give something, not take something.

Seeing my mother lying in the hospital with an ice pack on her chest the morning after her surgery, whispering for me to spoon feed her a few ice chips to soothe her ravaged throat (the result of jamming in, then yanking out a breathing tube) didn't make me say, "What am I doing with my life? Don't I realize what's important?" Rather, it calmed me, because I was there for her, I was there for my family. It told me to hold steady and be patient.

The whole mess got shoved into my writing. All fiction is memoir, and all memoir is fiction. Smart, writer-types are probably howling at that pronouncement, but it's true. Fiction is supposed to be something that imagined, but we can only fund our imagination through our perception of reality. You can't imagine something that you don't already have the elements of inside you. Fiction is the uniqueness each author brings to those elements of reality. And memoir is misleading. There's a notion that it's an accurate memory, and that is an oxymoron. No memory is accurate, unless it's transcribed and videotaped. Each person sees things differently, filtering them through our own point of view. Add the passage of time to the equation, and what makes it onto the page may be factually correct, but completely biased by the author's point of view, and therefore fictional.

I didn't write specifically about my mother's ordeal, but I did write about those feelings, that transformation that happened to her, and the result was a story called "Hands." At its core, "Hands" is about a family full of people consumed with their own needs. The mother develops breast cancer, has successful surgery, and recovers, and through her quiet, faithful journey the rest of the family settles into their final forms. Not everyone lands softly, and my point was to illustrate the messiness of life. Happy endings don't exist unless we tell them to exist.

§

By the time I graduated, I'd polished and revised my collection to a high tolerance. I submitted it for publication twice during the spring before I graduated. The first time it was rejected, but the second time, a small press in Maine called Dan River Press accepted it. As I said earlier, I had no delusions of commercial success, and neither did the publisher. One of his requirements was that I actively participate in the marketing of the book, and that took the shape of pre-sales. I think I managed to sell about 100 copies of the book before it went to press. From the point of view of the publisher, it wasn't a bad financial strategy. His reasoning was that in order to offer publication to work that was worthy, but that probably wouldn't generate a lot of sales, he had to raise money, and instead of raising the money after the publication of the book through sales, he found that most authors could generate more sales on the front end. And so it was with Name the Boy.

Depending on your point of view, the process of bringing a book to publication can waver between horrific and exhilarating. From a writer's point of view, it's trying. You just want the thing published. You don't want to deal with all the baloney: contracts, galleys, endless problems with cover art. You want to see your name emblazoned on something solid, something physical. And then, when it happens, you hate it. You find every little place where you failed as a writer, and you can't believe you wrote such garbage. You're humbled and ashamed, and now you have to put on a brave face and start promoting the thing. Smile! Buy my book!

For me, the most difficult part was engaging people about my work in a way that was honest, but which also promoted it to them. In other words, selling. I'm a bad salesman. In addition to the all the pre-selling of my book, I also came up with a few ways of marketing that were unique to me. For example, I added a link to the Auberge website promoting my book. I'd already had a link there for my blog, and now I added a promotional blurb:

> Your innkeeper, Shawn Kerivan, has written a book, a collection of short stories called Name the Boy. Shawn's book was published in the fall of 2006 by Dan River Press. To find out more, or to order a copy, click on the photo and visit Shawn's website.[7]

Beside the blurb was a picture of the book cover, which linked directly to my website. The website was really my storefront. Copies of my book could be bought there, and it linked back to the Auberge site. And that part of the marketing worked. Many guests arrive, and if I'm there to greet them, sometimes I see that look in their eyes as they glance from me to the shelves with my books on them, and back to me: Is that him? Sometimes they confess right away: "Oh, we've read your blog." Sometimes they even use the B-word: "Is that your book?" Me: "Yes." Them (nodding): "Wow." And that pretty much ends the conversation. See what I mean about being a lousy salesman?

There are authors out there who are great promoters of their own work. One writer, who came through Stowe and spoke, self-published his own book, a disjointed, rambling tome dealing with specialized and esoteric subject matter, sold tons of books. But he was dashing and a good speaker and salesman, and since people thought he sounded like he knew what he was talking about, they coughed up the twenty bucks for the book. I'm a good-looking guy, and a decent speaker, funny, a real character. But I don't turn it on and off on a whim. My humor and character are sincere, and I can't project them in any situation. And I don't have the relentless drive needed to organize a promotional tour and sell books. Those are my shortcomings, and I freely admit to them. I was also limited by an exhausting schedule, and a genuine indifference on the part of local venues, like libraries and radio stations, to leap at the chance to feature a local author. By the time I managed a reading at the Stowe Free Library—whose director had been one of my champions—it was a cold, dark November night, 8 months after the release of my book. Seventeen people showed up to the reading, and I sold four books.

This surprised me, especially given the amount of recognition I'd built up over the years in Stowe. I'd written a regular column about innkeeping for the Reporter for a year and a half, and people still remembered it and asked me about it. I'd also written a column the autumn before about the process of creating and publishing a book, called "An Author's Road." I even sent out a batch of postcard invitations to people, about twenty of them, telling them about the reading and asking if they could come. Not a single one of them showed up. And then there was the review published by the Reporter the week before the reading.

Accompanying the review was a biographical blurb talking about me, my writing for the Reporter, and highlighting the time and place for the reading. I was even billed as an "Writer-Innkeeper,"[8] which should have been unique enough to interest a few more people. But the review itself disappointed me. I was thrilled that I received so much space—an entire page of the newspaper was devoted to me—but the trade-off was the content. The reviewer struggled with the book, finding little redemption within the stories, as if that were an unstated goal for readers. After an opening paragraph quoting Henry David Thoreau talking about the misery of men's lives, the reviewer logged this enticing gem:

> Kerivan's characters live desperate lives, filled with fear, helplessness, anger and despair. It's a word (sic) of poverty and hard lives as fishermen or farmers, a world of abusive fathers, ineffective and/or drunken mothers and wives, tormented big brothers, and helpless younger siblings — a depressing world of people trapped in bad relationships, without laughter and with very little love.[9]

Just the kind of book you want to crawl up with in bed, huh? If that weren't enough, check out the list of atmosphere-creating vocabulary culled from the review: "hurt, frightening, violence, devouring, fighting, unbearable, pure horror, crude, cruel, monsters."[10] It's a list only Stephen King could love. What really peeved me was the reviewer's failure to see the immense humor laced throughout the book. Tragedy and humor are flip sides of the same coin, and while my book isn't as dark as King

Lear, it's full of hope and life—and love, and redemption, and reality, all of which weren't recognized. I can only attribute that to the limitations the reviewer brought to the reading of the book, and that's something a writer has to live with. I can say that my book has been recognized on a different level, and it's being taught in both literature and creative writing classes at the undergraduate level, which, in a twisted way, makes me more proud than tons of sales and stellar reviews.

But still...

The process marked me in ways I'll probably be discovering for years to come. It didn't deepen my cynicism, but it did heighten the peaks and lower the valleys. And it led to the writing of this book, and that led to my eventual departure from FedEx. The publication of Name the Boy also became a tool for my teaching career, for most college level positions as writing teachers require both an MFA and a published book. Of course, once you have those, you need to find a school that's actually hiring, and then you have the pleasure of competing against 12 million other applicants who, it turns out, are just as special as you. So I keep writing, and I begin here, locally, with the wonderful teaching opportunities that the Community College of Vermont has offered me—enough so that I was able to quit FedEx and do what I really wanted.

Chapter Seventeen
Sláinte! Prosit! Santé!

It always happens the same way. I don't want to stereotype, but I think it's justified here. A guest will check in during the afternoon, just as I'm returning from work at FedEx. I'll greet them, still bedecked in my FedEx uniform. And if they're of a generation above mine, they'll usually say something like, "Oh, you work for FedEx? They're a good outfit."

And, of course, they're right. FedEx is a good outfit to work for, if you like wearing outfits, and you like working. I like neither, which is why I'm a writer and an innkeeper. But the story of my involvement with FedEx, and how that involvement shaped our experience as innkeepers, is really the story of health insurance in America.

§

I had always wanted to work for FedEx. The whole notion of a group of people dedicated to service appealed to my sense of neatness, accomplishment. I liked the efficient look of the white trucks, the smart way the employees walked, the look of their purple-tailed white planes arrowing through the night, in and out of Memphis. Okay, the Memphis thing befuddled me at first, until I looked at a map of the country. Then I understood the importance of its location as a hub. And becoming a part of that organization contributed to a lot of the success I developed, both professionally as an innkeeper, and as a writer. Plus, there was the health insurance. When you're attached to an organization that offers your family comprehensive health insurance for $85 a month, everything's rosy. In fact, it's addictive, making every other option look crazy. So in January, 2008, when I left FedEx and jumped into the reality of health care in America, I had completed one odyssey, and I was about to embark on another.

Everybody knows FedEx. Depending on which report you read, FedEx is one of the most recognizable companies on the planet, standing shoulder to shoulder with the likes of Coca-Cola, McDonald's, and IBM. Their television commercials are legendary, beginning with the fast talker John Moschitta that introduced the world to the phrase, "When it absolutely, positively, has to be there overnight," up to the modern era, where their new motto, "Relax, it's FedEx," aims itself squarely at the small business owner. Of course, what FedEx was doing in its ads was engraining itself in the American popular culture psyche. And it worked.

My first personal brush with FedEx came in 1988, when a friend of mine named Kerri Darcey began dating a young man who worked for FedEx in Boston. Jimmy Seibel was quiet, professional, and confident, exactly the kind of profile I'd imagined for a FedEx employee. Even then, with the company only 15 years old, the FedEx ethos loomed large in America, and much of it can be traced to the history of its founder, Frederick W. Smith.

According to FedEx, the idea for the company began with a paper about the need for an air transportation system that could handle time-sensitive shipments in the modern age that Smith wrote while an undergraduate at Yale in 1965. While Smith only received a C on the paper, the idea stuck with him. After college, he entered the United States Marine Corps and became a pilot, serving in Vietnam. After the war, Smith realized his goal of starting his own company, and on April 17, 1973, Federal Express was born.[11]

I tried to get a job with FedEx in the early 90s, just after Chantal and I returned from France. But the economy was floundering, and FedEx was in the middle of a hiring freeze. Things were different in 1998, when, after three years in Montreal, we returned to the two-family house we owned in Braintree, Massachusetts. After 8 years in the corporate world, Chantal wanted to be home with the boys. So I called Jim, who was now married to Kerri and had a couple of kids, and asked about working for FedEx. Now a manager, Jim put me in touch with his brother Pete, also a manager, at the Randolph terminal, and on September 24, 1998, I was hired by FedEx.

The most tangible benefit for us was the health care package FedEx offered. With two small children to care for, that benefit can't be overstated. And it was that benefit that kept me with the company for ten years. When we decided to buy our bed and breakfast, the banker didn't blink when approving our loan; he saw that I was employed by FedEx, and that helped us realize the dream of becoming innkeepers.

I stayed with FedEx throughout our tenure as innkeepers for two reasons: first, the affordability of the health insurance; and second, the added income. Our first years in Vermont were not profitable; in fact, we ran the business at a loss. My income from FedEx was important to our business plan. Even when I transitioned to part-time, we kept our health benefits (FedEx extends the same health benefits to part-timers as they do to full-timers), and we kept nearly the same income (as a part-timer, I worked about 30 hours a week; as a full-timer, I worked around 40, sometimes a little less). For three years, the situation was ideal.

Then Goddard happened, and teaching opportunities began to open up for me exactly as increased volumes of packages shipped at Coffee (resulting in more physical exhaustion) hastened the formation of my exit strategy from FedEx. But there was still that nagging question of health insurance.

There is something insidious and insane going on in the United States. How is it that FedEx can offer me comprehensive health insurance for $160 a month (after ten years the price had doubled), but I can't buy into that plan on my own? The same plan, if bought privately, would cost over $1,000 a month. Say what? FedEx and Blue Cross (their provider) will smile and tell us proudly that because FedEx represents 180,000 employees, Blue Cross can offer them deep discounts. And all you have to do is work for FedEx. But what about the 300 million employees of the United States of America? Isn't that a big enough pool? Why can only large corporations be entrusted to manage and administer our access to health insurance? It smacks of corporate socialism and rubs up against fascism.

Imagine if I didn't have to work for FedEx to have access to the same health insurance I have when I'm working for them. Imagine if none of us had to work for specific companies to have access to their insurance plans. Imagine if we were free to choose a company based on its ability to provide us with the kind of job we've trained and studied for, not based on its benefits package. Imagine if the clerk at the quick mart was a single mother and she only had to pay $100 a month for health insurance, the same as the guy pumping gas into his Mercedes outside her window. Imagine a country where freedom of choice really means something; it's easy if you try.

Here's the reality: Companies like FedEx would lose one of their biggest competitive edges if health insurance were removed from the equation. Millions of Americans would be able to choose where they worked without having to evaluate how much they'd need to pay for health insurance. They'd still need to pay for their insurance, and they should; that should remain and individual choice for a customer to make between competing providers. But there's no logical reason why it should be tied to big business.

In fact, the entire history of health insurance in the United States is an exercise in ad hoc administration, like a child's Lego creation that's been added onto periodically, until it resembles something so bizarre, yet so reflective of our society, that we don't know what to do with it. And like a child, we've formed an irrational attachment to it. We lack the maturity to give it up and move on. Instead, we scream and cry when we realize it's time to put the toys away.

More than 60 percent of Americans receive their health insurance through their employers. This means that the other 40 percent—120 million men, women, and children—have to look somewhere else for health insurance. If they don't qualify for Medicaid or Medicare, they will either pay for it themselves, or go without. And go without they do. A 2002 estimate put the number of uninsured in America at around 40 million. We are the only major industrialized nation on the planet that runs thing this way.[12] But you've heard that already. The bigger question is, So what?

Well, here's what. We live in an insurance-driven nation. Forty years ago, neither my parents, nor anybody else they knew, had insurance, except where it was mandated. The state told them they had to have insurance for their car, and the bank told them they had to have insurance for their house (actually the insurance was for the money they borrowed to buy the house, not the house itself). But they didn't have health insurance. And when something went wrong, when someone was sick or injured? They paid for it. If they didn't have the money, they borrowed it. And, of course, medical expenses weren't as high then, even relatively speaking, even adjusted for 1964 dollars, or whatever that hocus-pocus is that economists are always doing to obfuscate the truth.

I'm not suggesting that we return to that level of living. We've evolved considerably since then. Some may say we've evolved too much or too fast, and that we spend our lives managing our children's development. Indeed it seems like many parents pursue business degrees just for that purpose, and the world is full of helicopter mothers, hovering a few feet from their children, protecting and correcting everything from their first steps to their first sexual encounter. But the mandate on safety and the financial punishment that's meted out to those who can't afford to buy into the system is truly one of the most unjust things ever to be codified by this country. It's downright Dickensian. As an example I offer my ten-year run at FedEx, and the transition we had to make when I left the company.

For as long as I worked at FedEx, my benefits package insulated us from the scary world of insurance, health and otherwise. The great thing about a company like FedEx is that I could multi-task my life without doing a thing—except reporting for work each day. I could fund my 401k, invest in my future, and receive a variety of coverage—medical, dental, vision, automobile—all by spending a few minutes each year enrolling in the various plans the company offered. That part of the job was alluring and numbing, a Siren's song. And for a small business owner, it was more. It gave us freedom from stress, and freedom from financial outlays that could have jeopardized the business, especially in the early years.

It was that benefits package that kept me with FedEx for as long as I stayed, for I'd become disenchanted with the company much earlier. The first blow came when I transferred up to the station in Williston. I went from a fast paced, semi-urban setting, full of dynamic characters and fluidity, to a recalcitrant, in-bred location, where the plane that flew our overnight freight in each morning was perpetually late, where the weather pushed the driving conditions beyond nightmarish and into dangerous, and where dour atmosphere cycled upon itself endlessly. I wasn't much help. I agitated for part-time status, then dug my heels in whenever extra work was heaped on my plate. I resented the expectation that if the station needed me, I'd have to stay and work extra that day, or that week. And if they didn't need me, they sent me home. I felt I was as flexible as I could be: I could work anytime between six in the morning and noon. During peak times, I came in earlier and stayed later. But it was never enough. The same situation evolved at Green Mountain Coffee Roasters. My supervisor constantly asked me to work extra, and I constantly said no.

What changed for us at the inn was our ability to make more money than we spent. Once that happened, I began to see a way to end my tenure at FedEx. By combining my new and expanding role as a teacher with the momentum of the inn, I was able to finally leave FedEx.

That leap away from corporate management of my health care plopped me in the middle of the mess this country has made for itself. It was a decision that involved heaping portions of consternation and aggravation. My original intent had been to quit back in the summer, at the end of August. Chantal and I had several conversations, and we decided that the inn was doing well enough so that I could just focus on teaching and writing. I'd been anxious to finish this book. Since I only had about four hours a week to work on it, it was crawling along. I even typed up my letter of resignation. But at the last minute, we both got cold feet. So I decided to stay through the fall and leave after Thanksgiving. But as that time drew near, and we talked about it again, we thought it might be a good idea to stay through the winter. What really happened is that I'd been hoping the Community College of Vermont (CCV)—one of the places where I teach—would offer me at least two classes for the spring semester. That would seal the deal for us, because it would replace more than the income I'd be giving up, giving us a little cushion to absorb the added expense of paying for our own insurance. But when CCV only offered me one class, quitting didn't seem like a viable idea, even though I was also teaching at the Mt. Mansfield Winter Academy (MMWA). So we thought we'd wait until spring.

I'd have to quit in the spring for sure, because I had several major projects lined up around here. The two big ones were rehabbing Room 1, and painting the building. I could probably start the Room 1 job in April, but the painting would have to wait till the end of May. Both would have to be finished by the middle of June. There's no way I could keep the job at FedEx and get that done the way it needed, and teach—though the semester runs only through the first week of May.

But then, just after Thanksgiving, the academic coordinator at the CCV campus in Montpelier called and offered me two English Comp classes for the spring semester. That meant I'd be teaching three college courses, plus three afternoons a week at MMWA. In the end, the decision was easy. I decided to stay with FedEx through Christmas—I couldn't leave before Christmas, right in the middle of the busiest time of the year, even though that meant I'd take a physical beating. On 28 December 2007 I gave notice to my supervisor that I'd be leaving FedEx on 11 January 2008. I was finally closing the book on FedEx.

Meanwhile, Chantal was thrown into a dither. The obvious hurdle for us was arranging health insurance immediately. But we also needed to schedule any visits to the dentist, especially for the boys, as well as figure where we were going to get our car insurance from (our automobile insurance was part of the insurance package through FedEx). There were several options. First was simply going to Blue Cross and buying a plan. But we belonged to several other organizations that offered health plans to their members, including the Stowe Area Association (SAA), where Chantal was a trustee. And since she's also a French national, she qualified for an ex-patriot insurance program subsidized by the French government. But I didn't.

We finally settled on the plan offered through SAA. The boys would go onto the Vermont state health insurance program offered to all children under 18, called Dr. Dynasaur. Having made the decision, the hard part came next. Our business structure complicated things immensely. And the forms that we needed to fill out didn't always fit our needs. We weren't just another family; we were a small business. Showing the different forms of income we had became a nightmare, and the application process dragged on. One of the things that drove us crazy was that none of the applications were for people who were about to lose their coverage, or would need coverage in the future. They were for people who had no coverage, which meant that we'd have to wait until our insurance lapsed in order to fill out the forms truthfully. It was maddening.

Vermont has managed to become a conservatively progressive state, a place of seeming paradoxes where differing ideas coexist. For example, the state offers subsidized health insurance for anyone uncovered. This plan, called Catamount Health, came into existence under one of the most pro-business, Republican governors in the country, Jim Douglas. It's amazing that in a state where hunting is enshrined in the state constitution, there's also a vein of progressive thought that rivals the Californias and Massachusettses. Unfortunately for us, we don't qualify for Catamount. Not because we don'e meet the income requirements—you only need to come under the 300% of the poverty level line to get into the program, and we're within that limit. The reason we don't qualify is because you have to have been without health insurance for at least one year to be eligible for Catamount Health. The logic behind this is that people would leave their enslaved jobs in droves if they could simply sign up for this plan. Duh. It's a clause only a moron could have gotten inserted into the plan. It makes no sense. While the stated goal of the plan is to immediately bring the uninsured into coverage, it ignores the real problem: selling your professional soul for health insurance. There are thousands of people working in this state just for health insurance, at jobs they despise. It's another example of the choke hold big business has over the government, another example of corporate welfare that actually stifles our system of free enterprise.

Imagine what American companies would be able to do if they were freed from the constraints of providing costly health insurance for their employees. They'd be able to compete globally with other nations whose companies aren't responsible for health coverage for their employees, that's what. The simple truth is that we pay for health care in some form, either through taxes or through inflated premiums. But we've heard that all before. We just haven't done anything about it.

Because of the complexity involved with our business structure, the stress level ratcheted up abnormally. Neither our accountant nor the insurance agent we contacted could give us a straight answer about how we should go about getting our insurance. The problem rested in the fact that we have never paid ourselves a salary, so we were unsure as to how we should pay for the insurance. Could we write checks directly from our business account? Or should we write checks from savings? The tax ramifications of the decision could be crippling.

The whole situation with not paying ourselves seems strange on the surface, but it was logical to us. In the beginning, there was no money, so it wasn't an issue. My earnings from FedEx covered our normal expenses—namely groceries and gas. As we began to realize more success and accumulate some excess money, we sunk it back into the business, revamping rooms, replacing heating systems that conked out, insulating parts of the building that needed it. Then we leased a vehicle. Finally, when it became evident that I'd be leaving FedEx, we conceded the need to pay ourselves a salary. The problem with all this money moving is that each time you shake things up, you're exposed to taxes.

If it sounds like I'm waffling between social liberalism and fiscal conservatism, you're right. That's another consequence of the predatory system we're faced with: we have to pick our way through tangled forest of rules and regulations, and missteps can result in financial hardship. It forces small business people to adopt an aggressive posture and it gnaws away at the fabric of community, reducing us to a gang of selfish islands out only for ourselves. Sigh.

In case things weren't convoluted and stressful enough, on the first Sunday after I left FedEx, while we were all up skiing, two of the boys' friends broke their arms on the slopes. I remember thinking, "Jeez, I'm not sure this is such a good idea." But later that week, when I called the

Vermont Office of Health Access, I was told that coverage for the boys under the Dr. Dynasaur program was retroactive for up to three months prior to the date the policy becomes active. In case of some emergency, we'd be covered. Seamus and I celebrated by getting sick with a stomach flu.

§

The InnSights article that preceded this chapter reflected an event that weighed heavily on our minds as we tried to figure out what to do about our insurance/work dilemma. That little faux pas on the slopes would have cost us over ten thousand dollars out of pocket had we not been properly insured. It was a scary moment, and it illustrates just what people go through, and just what we're stuck with. At least for now.

Chapter Eighteen
A Business Matures

Every once in a while we get a request for something not apparent, something we might not have thought of. When we first put up our website, one request we received fairly often was for pictures of the rooms. Sometimes people would call and ask for us to describe the rooms—and that still happens, usually for one of two reasons: the first is because there are sleeping arrangements that need to be made. For example, if two couples are traveling together, they might want to know how the two-bedroom suite is configured. Or a family might want to know the same thing to figure out who's going to sleep where. It's a logistical thing. The second reason people ask for room descriptions sets off alarms.

We don't pretend to be a luxury B&B. Our prices reflect that. The information on our website reflects that. The Continental breakfast reflects that. And yet some people persist in making us into that. We do our best to ruin their image of us before they book, but sometimes they want to know what the rooms look like, and the line of questioning usually goes like this:

"Could you describe the room to me?"

"Well, it's got a bed, a couple of windows, and a bathroom."

"Is the bathroom private?"

"If you close the door, I suppose."

"What kind of a bed is it?"

"The mattress kind."

"I mean what size."

"It's a queen size."

"Does the room have a fireplace in it?"

"No."

"How about a Jacuzzi tub?"

"No, but we have an outdoor hot tub."

"How big is the room?"

"Hold on, please."

...(five minutes pass)...

"Still there? It's 11'6" by 14'8"."

"How high—"

"Seven feet."

"So—"

"One thousand, one hundred and sixty-seven and a quarter cubic feet."

"Okay. So, let me see, um, how would you describe the room."

(At this point my lip's bleeding from my teeth sinking through. I'm dying to say something like, "It's got a floor and four walls and a ceiling," but I think that might blow my cover. Actually, what I want to say is "It's decorated in early modern go-to-hell." But that won't work either. So I've got to figure out a way to get them off the phone ASAP, because the ice is melting in my drink.)

"You know, we're really not a fancy place, we just try to keep things simple so that we can offer people good value in Stowe, where everything is very expensive. It doesn't sound like we'd be the right place for you to stay, but I can give you the names of a couple of places that have the kinds of accommodations you're looking for."

I've found that you can only go so far with cheeky, especially in this age of instant communication, where it's easy for people to badmouth you, even when it's not the innkeeper's fault. So exchanges like the one above are becoming rarer, which is a shame, because that kind of stuff added a lot of sport to an otherwise subdued profession.

We've started to get Internet versions of this exchange, however.

Just before Christmas, a man called to book one of the suites for him and his friends in March. He explained that there were four of them, and that they took a ski trip together every year, and this year they were coming to Stowe. Great! So his questions were of the logistical nature: bed configuration, bathroom location, etc. All good. Then he asked if there was a picture of the room, because there wasn't a photo of that suite on the website. He and his friends just wanted to get an idea of the rooms, he explained. Fussy old guys, he said.

I told him the rooms were occupied through the holidays, but that I'd get in there after and take a couple of photos and email them to him. Splendid! January comes, and we get an email from the gentleman reminding us of the need for pictures. Right! I get in the rooms with my digital camera and blaze away. The pictures actually look good, and I figure I'll put them up on the website (although I'm sure people will ask if we have any other pictures of the rooms). Chantal emails the pictures to the fellow with this attached note:

> Good morning and Happy New Year! Funny I was just thinking I needed to get on this. Shawn just uploaded those photos last week

and you've been very patient. Thank you.

Chantal

But wait! There's more! Of course he emails us right back, and this is what he says:

> Thanks however these pictures were taken Halloween according to the info you sent to me. You must have something a little more appealing showing how the rooms are connected and more current. I don't want to be a "pain" however the other gentlemen won't really appreciate these pictures. Please send something more appealing. Again not be be a pain but... Later

Huh? What? I felt like I was just sucker punched. More appealing? Did he want to see girls in bikinis reclining on the beds? I shook the cobwebs from my head and conferred with Chantal. The Halloween part befuddled me. The pictures were taken in January, but when they were uploaded onto the computer, they were bundled with the previous photos on the camera, which were taken on Halloween, and somehow were given the file name "Halloween.jpg." There weren't pumpkins or goblins in the rooms when I took the pictures. He was being a pain. Here's what I wrote back to him:

> The photos were taken last week, and I'm afraid to say that's the best I can do for you. Each room has a queen bed and a single bed in it, with a connecting door and a bathroom between them. The rooms are on the first floor of the building. If you don't think the rooms are suitable, perhaps you should look around for other accommodations. Whatever you decide, please keep us informed.
> Thanks,
> Shawn

This is an example of me trying to cheerfully suggest that he go to hell. What's happening here is that my hourly rate is plummeting. The amount of time it's taking us to complete this deal is going up, but the room rate stays the same. Now I've explained again, in writing, the same thing we discussed on the phone, and it's starting to look like they shouldn't be staying with us. If they require this much maintenance two months before their scheduled arrival, I'm terrified to think what they'll be like when they get here. What if it rains? What if the ambience isn't right? What if monkeys fly out of my butt while they're checking in? This is what he writes back:

> Hello,
>
> On Dec 12, 2007 I recieved [sic] confirmation on our reservations for March 6-9th Assigned to suite 2-3 for 3 adult males. A special request was made to you to take a picture or pictures of the suite. However at the time of the request you stated it was being renovated /carpets and you would send a picture later once work was completed. When I recieved [sic] your previous email it had pictures of what appears to be your other rooms not the reserved suite. Just a request. We plan on seeing you in March. Thanks again.

Just a request. And we never stated it was being renovated. The rooms were occupied, then being cleaned, and we didn't have time to drop everything and take pictures and email them right away. Life was happening. And why would I send him pictures of rooms that he didn't reserve? Where did that come from, and how would he know? As my dear brother-in-law (who is an old Signal Corps guy in he Army) would say: "What the fuck! Over!"

The most frustrating part of this is that we feel we're being unnecessarily poked. It still confounds me how, upon seeing the pictures, he didn't say, "Well, here are the rooms," and then decide that he either liked them, or didn't like them, and acted from there. The gentleman obviously felt snubbed, and we were peeved. And it all comes down to expectations, expectations on our part that potential guests will evaluate us on the information we give them, expectations on the part of our potential guests that they choose the place that suites them best. The balancing act for us becomes a question of how we can distinguish ourselves and attract the kind of guest to our inn that we want to have staying here without sounding obsequious or nuts.

§

One of the things that allows us to operate from a position of confidence is experience. The other is lack of debt. While we haven't made millions as innkeepers, it's cost us almost nothing. We're beholden only to ourselves, and that gives us an ability to deal with people on a more honest level. If the situation described above had happened within the first few years of our innkeeping, we certainly would have behaved differently, but mostly out of fear, not opportunity. Now we recognize instantly that guests who begin agitating well before their stay are to be avoided; back then we would have said or done almost anything to get him in the door. And then we would have suffered.

It's always been important to us for our guests to understand that we're not here to pamper them, to fawn over them, to tell them what they want to hear. It may sound counterintuitive, but the customer isn't always right. The trick is to let them discover that. But some people can never be disabused of the notion that because they're paying money, they deserve to be treated differently. Instead, we try to treat all people with dignity and respect, whether they've paid for a three-night stay, or they're just replenishing the brochures in the lobby.

Maturity is the key. It's a subject that's tricky to elaborate on without being cliché. There's the maturity we've reached as individuals, as parents, and as husband and wife. There's the maturity the inn—the business—has reached. And there's the maturity our guests have reached, for many of them have seen our website or driven by the inn many times, and our endurance has edified us within their minds. I try to convey a little of that maturity through my blog, which I hope people glance at when they're visiting our website. That maturity informs our decisions, even as the constants of the business change again.

I realize the inherent contradiction in what I just said: how can something be constant if it changes? But it's really just another way of brining up the subject of fixed costs: fuel, electricity, water, the mortgage. Things like that never go away, impervious to the demands of the current economy. But their costs fluctuate, and as far as I can tell, only in one direction: up. And there's one spot where we see a strange phenomenon: the price of gas.

When we came to Stowe, gas was $1.50 per gallon. It was significantly cheaper in Braintree, Massachusetts, where we lived, because just down the street in Quincy was the depot where all the refined gasoline for the region entered. There were several small, independent gas stations in the area that offered gas at two-thirds the national average. By the end of 2004, the screaming began, and gas prices edged up over $2.00 per gallon. When that happened, some people in the tourist industry in Stowe overreacted. Businesses began offering gas cards to guests as a way to entice potential visitors. As the price of gas steadily climbed, those offers—largely psychological balms—went away. And in late 2007 we began to endure gas prices above $3.00 a gallon.[13] Yet we had one of our busiest falls ever, and the books were filled for the winter, which is even more amazing when you consider the price of a lift ticket in Stowe is $79, $84 during holidays. And to confuse things further, when gas hit $4 a gallon this spring, we had our best June since we opened our doors. So what's the deal? How can a place like the Auberge, which advertises itself as "affordable in Stowe" weather something that should be crippling its target demographic?

There are a couple of things at work here, one you already know, and one you don't. The first is the concept of adjusted income. The government explains it by saying "energy expenditures relative to disposable income for the average consumer is less than the historic peak."[14] And the historic peak for relative gas prices was in the early 1980s. That calculation also takes into account the notion that Americans have more disposable income in 2007 than they had 25 years earlier, but that's debatable. In any case, that's the party line.

The other thing is what I call price shifting. While our room rate in Stowe is at the lower end of the range, in the larger range of prices throughout the country, we're middle of the road, about twice as much as bargain accommodations, and half as much as luxury. Being in the middle is good because it insulates you from extremes. So while we may lose people who looked to us to gain affordable access to a room in Stowe, we're gaining people who may have spent more in the past, but are feeling the economic pinch a little more than before. They're the people who, in the past, may have overspent a little and upgraded to a luxury place. Now they're looking for a different value. And if fuel prices decline, we'll gain back the other folks we lost to higher gas prices.

This theory isn't foolproof, especially when I'm the fool proposing it. It's based on conversation and anecdote, on observation, and profiling our customers. It's the synthesis of time and theory. The flaw in this thinking is that Stowe is a luxury destination, and with the new unabashedly upscale development at the base of the mountain, it's pricing itself ever higher. Say gas prices decline. Could those customers of ours who used to come up here looking for a $75 a night room afford to come back? After all, we've increased our room rates to around $90 a night. Presumably they would. They'd view the money they're no longer spending on higher fuel prices as disposable, and I'm the guy holding out the trashcan.

Anybody who speaks in terms of absolutes is a fool. Nobody is insulated from the pains of the economy, and nobody has figured out a way to succeed. Innkeeping is an inexact science, and in fact it should remain that way. It's more of a calling, a vocation, than it is something to build a future on. In fact, the success in innkeeping isn't about building up a business that will sustain you profitably in the years to come, something that you can sell for a gain. It's a real estate project. Turning a building into an inn—or building a new one from scratch—is all about property improvement. You start your inn, make improvements, and wait for time to do its little dance with real estate prices. Those who are in it for the long term—at least ten years—can withstand the economic cycles of boom and bust. And then, when and if you sell, you're selling an improved piece of property with the cachet of a dream splashed across it. The innkeeping business won't make you money, but the real estate will.

Of course, this isn't absolute. The guy who has to beg, borrow, and steal to get his inn going is going to be more exposed to the rigors of the fickle economy. If he times it right, he'll get his tough years under his belt during a boom cycle, and be prepared to weather the downturns. But if he blinks, he's cooked. If he has his own sugar daddy, a family money pump that infuses him with cash at critical junctures, or some other external money source, he'll stand a better chance of survival.

§

After eight years of innkeeping, we've begun to really think about the future. A lot has changed for us in the last year. I've quit FedEx, the inn is beginning to pay for not only itself, but lots of other things. The boys are in middle school, and we've begun thinking about options for the high school years. And the economy's going into the toilet again. We're not sure we want to be innkeepers for another eight years. Then again, we're not sure we don't want to be, either.

Earlier this winter, we went to a house auction. It was a great place, an unfinished, cedar log sided house on 20 acres of land in Johnson, Vermont. The work remaining to be done was mostly interior finish work. We envisioned it as vacation rental property in the short term, with us possibly moving there in the medium to long term. One of the plans we're thinking of with the inn is to lease it out to an aspiring innkeeper, with an option to buy. I'd love to get full-time work at Johnson State College, in the BFA in Creative Writing program. A decent salary would be nice, and it would give us more flexibility in our decision-making. We could also sell the Auberge—not as an inn, of course, but as commercial property. The Lower Village of Stowe has been experiencing a makeover, with more businesses moving here, and the value of our property has increased steadily. Then again, we could remain here and just chug along. We're good at that, and it's a nice life.

Shawn Kerivan

Chapter Nineteen
The Naughty Bits

Soon after we had the hot tub installed on the back deck, in the fall of 2001, people began taking advantage of it. Since it was a new system within the inn, we needed to get used to its routine. There was the usual chemistry involved, but there were mechanical systems as well, like a pump with a thermostat attached, and a cover that folded back upon itself and slid onto a pair of supports. One thing we noticed quickly was that people didn't always button it back up when they were finished using it. In the winter, when it's 5 degrees outside, that could be a problem. So before I went to bed each night that fall, I got into the habit of checking the hot tub, making sure that the cover was on properly, and that the pump was turned off.

One Friday night I made my way toward the back room, only to be halted in my tracks by a rhythmic chugging sound that wasn't the water jets. It was late, near 11, and I still wasn't used to the workings of the hot tub. But the couple that was in there when I came around the corner seemed to have figured things out just fine. Madame had her bikini top wrapped around her neck, and Monsieur's trunks were floating several feet away. They were having a contest with the bubbles to see who could move the fastest in a random motion. It was the first time I'd ever caught anybody in flagrante delicto, but I didn't need a copy of the Kama Sutra to figure out what was going on. I retreated discreetly and allowed realization to dawn on me. I also made a mental note to change the water before I used the hot tub again.

§

The prudishness of Americans amazes me. I include myself in that accusation, too. We're uncomfortable with topics that aren't rated G. Even PG gets our blood racing. On the outside, we're champions of propriety, wholesomeness, and decency. Yet we're the home to the porn industry that sets a ribald tone for the rest of the world. It's obvious that we're very uncomfortable with our sexuality. As the owner of a business that measures its success on how many people it can put into bedrooms, I understand a few things about people's habits in strange beds. First, there are only three things people do in beds: Sleep, not have sex, and have sex.

There's a certain excitement to traveling: senses are stimulated in new ways, awareness is heightened. Add to that the celebratory nature of traveling—eating out at a nice restaurant, shopping—and the pheromones are released by the bagful. It doesn't take much to go from prudish to prurient; I know, I've seen the evidence. What's astonishing is that we don't even advertise ourselves as a "romantic" inn. Sometimes I think that if all we rented were tent sites in the back yard I'd still be dealing with the aftermath of boy meets girl. I've met a lot of innkeepers who advertise themselves as "romantic getaways," and I always wonder if they understand fully what they're doing, if they understand that "romantic" is more than just some marketing catch phrase, something to increase occupancy. In this business, romantic is an adjective that means "place to go have sex." But then again, we're talking about Americans here, champions of exuding propriety and purity on the outside, whips and chains on the inside.

The notion of a romantic weekend, or a romantic getaway always amused me. Being more of a realist, I appreciate the British term for it: dirty weekend. In America, the romantic getaway traveler spends gobs of money on some lavishly appointed room decorated with lavender and muted yellows, then spends gobs of money on a meals and a bottle of wine, and then retreats to the four-poster canopy bed with the gaudy throw pillows and makes love. In England one runs off to the Midlands for a dirty weekend, nips into the local pub for a bite and a pint, then retreats to Mrs. Thornbury's upstairs bedroom for a shag.

It's not the part of the traveler that makes me shake my head in this scenario; it's the innkeeper. A brief Internet search of "romantic inns" will return bazillions of hits. We're awash in them. In fact, it's almost as if they're crucial to repopulation efforts. The whole notion of romance in America has been replaced with an exoskeleton of marketing contrivances like silk sheets and fireplaces in the bedroom and Jacuzzi tubs in the bathroom. The notion that a jetted tub for two in a bathroom—the place where you, ahem, take care of business—is romantic is beyond laughable. Imagine snuggling among the bubbles with your significant other, a few feet from Thomas P. Crapper's namesake. Scintillating.

Yet this is just the thing that the savvy innkeeper will strive for, because that's where the money is. It's that need for external stimuli that creates this glut of upscale inns positioning themselves as romantic destinations. As long as there's an America where sexuality is repressed and violence is celebrated, there'll be a huge market for romantic destinations. Of course, you don't have to market yourself as a romantic inn to draw the crowds. Just as Mrs. Thornbury in the Midlands will tell you, the overwhelming desire of humans to share confined spaces infiltrates every level of innkeeping, including ours at the Auberge.

§

Innkeepers should never be surprised that guests are having sex in the hot tub, or anywhere else. Chantal and I have adopted a very European approach to this at the Auberge, especially within the context of the hot tub. We've even gone so far as to create a document that explains the workings of the hot tub, and how we'd like people to use it. One of the things that peeves us is having people go in the hot tub with street clothes—namely, their underwear, or a t-shirt, or some other garment that isn't a bathing suit. The problem with this is that those clothes get washed in a washing machine, and there's always soap residue left on them. Putting them back into a container of warm water that's being agitated by a series of water jets releases the soap that wasn't rinsed out—and American style washing machines do a poor job at rinsing and wringing clothes. That turns the hot tub into a giant bubble bath, frothing over and creating a mess. We tell people that we've got a box of bathing suits they can borrow if needed, or that they can go in naked. It's up to them. Some people, especially Europeans, don't need any encouragement.

During one Christmas week, when the inn was full, we had a situation that reflected the eclectic nature of the place. There was an English family staying with us, a couple with a little boy who must have been about 5. They had their day of skiing, and had returned to the inn to relax in front of the fire and play some board games. We also had a young couple from somewhere in Eastern Europe staying with us. They, too, had their day of skiing, and were relaxing in the hot tub. It was about four in the afternoon.

Hearing some activity in the back room, I wandered back to say hello, see how the English folks were doing, ask if they needed anything. I heard the hot tub going, but I didn't wander over to the slider door to see who was in it. As I was talking to the parents of the little boy, he suddenly interrupted us. He was standing in front of the slider, pointing outside, and he said, "Mummy, there are naked people out there." The English folks, to their credit, were typically British in their understated reaction. The father looked up and said, "Yes, so there are. I think it's your move, darling." The mother looked up from the board game she was playing, too, and said, "Don't point, love. It's not polite." Then she turned back to her game.

The innkeeper's husband showed no such decorum. Being a sexually repressed American, he scurried to the window, where the little boy was still standing. And there, indeed, were naked people. The young couple was standing outside, next to the hot tub, toweling off, in no particular rush to robe themselves. In the interest of the writing of this book, I observed the scene carefully. Strangely, I felt no titillation. Perhaps it was their plank-like twentysomething bodies, or perhaps it was that by the ripe old age of forty I'd seen plenty of naked people, and two more, standing outside next to a hot tub, were just clinical at that point. The couple looked up and, seeing me, smiled and waved. Emboldened, I opened the slider and stuck my head out.

"How was the skiing?" I asked.

"Fantastic," they replied, in heavily accented, but otherwise perfect English. (It always astounds me how hard the rest of the world works to speak other languages, yet Americans reject linguistics as something unholy. That attitude, I mused, makes us lazy and vulnerable, for we are far from the most intelligent people on the planet.)

"It snowed the entire day," continued the fellow. "We skied in the woods."

"Yes," his mate added with enthusiasm. "Stowe has so many places in the woods to ski. It's very natural."

So it is, I agreed. They put their robes on, replaced the cover on the hot tub, and went back to their room, saying hello to the English folks as they passed by. The English couple asked them how the hot tub was, and when they replied positively, the English lady said to her husband, "We should go in. Perhaps after dinner?" He replied, "Perhaps, indeed," and I thought I saw a sly smile spread across his face as I left.

§

I'm sure there have been many more moments au naturel that I've missed. And I'm sure that many of our guests have fond memories of naughty moments stolen late at night, under the stars. Nakedness and the prelude to love-making (there I go again with my prudishness—why can't I just say sex?) are fun and playful, or at least they should be. It's what people are looking for when they think about getting away—whether that means a romantic retreat or a dirty weekend. But there's a flip side to the exciting moments engendered between the sheets. Of course, I'm talking about body fluids.

The inability to talk about the stuff that falls out of, leaks out of, projects forth from, and seeps from within humans remains as prudish and infantile as the unwillingness to discuss sex frankly. But dealing with those indelicacies constitutes a large part of an innkeeper's day. So steel yourself and read on; I won't tell you anything you don't already know, and I'll try to be grown up and funny about it, so that when you grimace and your skin tingles you'll at least be happy about it. Let's start with the hot tub.

Here's a rule I've adopted that might surprise you: never let the Irish into your hot tub. They're consistently destructive, and I've yet to figure out why. We don't have many visitors to Stowe from Ireland (except the three Irish ladies from Northern Ireland who shared an entire bottle of Lagavulin with me), and maybe they just lose their minds in the cold. But the Irish we've had at the Auberge have been daffy. One group, here for a wedding, went into the hot tub fully clothed. Why they didn't disrobe is a mystery I'm blaming on the Catholic Church and Jamesons Irish Whiskey. I'm not sure what they spilled in there, but they ruined the water beyond repair, turning it green and foamy, with floating chunks riding the bubbles like the ship of the Ancient Mariner. Since it happened late at night, and they were wearing all their clothes, I suspect that chunks were blown. All I remember is that I needed a shovel after I drained the water, and I found shoe at the bottom.

Most of all, merry-making at the inn victimizes the sheets. Entering rooms each morning to make beds becomes a non-lethal form of Russian roulette. Let me amend that: it may not be lethal to your physical health, but mentally you suffer. Many a morning Chantal and I have whipped back the covers as we've started to make a bed, only to be halted in our tracks by devastation. While it may not be surprising to discover the evidence of the dirty deed imprinted onto the cloth, the exact location of the stain is amusing. We've found them up on pillow cases, along the edge of the mattress, and even on the floor. Dissecting the scene puts us in the shoes of forensic experts: CSI: Stowe.

"That's a good one," I said of one unlikely mark. "How do you suppose they managed to get it way up there?"

Chantal cocked her head to one side and thought about it. Her eyes darted up to the ceiling, which slanted down toward the head of the bed. She calculated time and distance, then shook her head. "Without dislocating something, I don't know." If only that was the worst thing with which we had to contend.

Aside from deliberately expelling fluids from their bodies, people also leak. This leaking is akin to the hair shedding described at the beginning of the book: it is relentless and unaccountable, and it wrecks sheets, mattress pads, and bedspreads. Some stains are identifiable; others defy explanation. Among the more common are snot, drool, piss, shit, blood, semen, toe jam, belly-button lint, earwax, dingleberries, eye crud, vomit, and bile. Of these, most disturbing is blood.

Everybody drools, farts get away from us sometimes, and sneezes empty the head of viscous liquid. But humans are usually attuned to losing blood; uncontrolled bleeding is dangerous. It's one thing to scratch a cut in your sleep; it's quite another to bleed enough to ruin several layers of bedding. And yet that's exactly what we've discovered some mornings while making beds. The bizarre thing is that the folks that were bleeding never seemed bothered when they were down at breakfast. Did they think the maid wouldn't say anything to us? Did they know that we were the maid?

As Chantal delicately puts it, "There are products designed especially for that kind of situation. My sheets aren't one of them." It's hard to imagine an adult tying a sheet through the saddle to stanch the flow, but it's true. Situations like that make other stains laughable. What people have left behind, including their stains, has a chilling effect on innkeepers, and we're not shy about sharing our stories with each other. Every innkeeper we know has experienced this horror.

On the lighter side, few innkeepers have discovered something as racy as a former innkeeper friend of ours did one morning while doing the housekeeping. Tom and Betty—not their real names—ran a lovely inn for several years until they sold it and headed south. We hung out together occasionally, and Betty was always willing to regale us with stories from her innkeeping adventures. But one topped them all. They had a nice couple staying with them for a few days, in the master suite. Fairly innocuous, until after the couple checked out, and Betty was cleaning the room. One thing an innkeeper always does is check under the bed. We've discovered everything from shoes to phones to money, but nothing like Betty's discovery. Under the bed that morning was a shoe box. She pulled it out and opened it and her jaw dropped. Instead of a pair of Ferragamo pumps she found a collection of sex toys: vibrators, dildos, assorted rings, ticklers...a veritable adult novelty store.

Because we innkeepers live for this kind of thing, Betty was excited. But there was a problem: what to do with the stuff? Should she call the people who left it behind: "Hi, this is Betty, you folks forgot all your sex toys, should I mail them back to you? And by the way, where did you get that double-ended dildo? I've been looking for one of those for ages." Or should she sit on it, so to speak, and wait for the couple to call. While she was debating, they called.

"Um, hi, this is _____, we stayed with you over the weekend? Yeah, well, I think we left something behind."

Betty: "You may have. Can you describe it for me?"

"Um, yeah, it was, like a shoe box kind of thing."

Betty: "A shoe box? Oh, sure, I found it. Doesn't sound like there are shoes in it, though. Something's rattling around in there."

"Um, yeah, well, we were kind of wondering if you could mail it back to us. We'd be happy to pay the postage. If it's not too much bother."

Betty: "Oh, gosh no. But it sounds like there's a lot of loose stuff inside there. Would you like me to repack it? I could stuff some bubble wrap in there. As a matter of fact, I'm surprised you haven't thought of stuffing bubble wrap in there already. You've thought of everything else."

With that they demurred, and Betty released them from her grip, and promised to mail it along. But not before she shared the episode with us. Whether the traveler views this as a cautionary tale should be up to him or her. If sex toys are important to the comfort of your stay, by all means bring them. But please make sure you check under the bed before you go.

Chapter Twenty
The Cult of Innkeeping

Everything comes back to high school. No matter where you are, no matter how far you advance in life, every social dynamic you insert yourself into becomes just another high school social scenario. We are all damned to find ourselves standing at the front of the cafeteria, lunch tray in our hands, surveying the layout of tables before us, filled with different cliques and societies of people, subgroups within subgroups, each bristling with exaggerated identities. Which to choose?

So it is with Stowe, and so it is within the innkeeping community in Stowe. There are factions and groups and cliques that reflect the social rules laid down in high school fabulosus, the hierarchies that govern...well, I don't know, something. That whole social posturing thing is anathema to me. But it still exists. People still judge you by the car you drive, the clothes you wear, the company you keep. These are ancient and immutable impulses, survival techniques bred into humans over millennia. In the olden days, telling the group to go to hell could get you dead. Now it's a matter of choice.

There are many ways to divide Stowe, and they all overlap. For instance, there are the natives, and the newcomers. Where that line falls depends on who you talk to. I know one woman who advertises herself as a "seventh generation Vermonter." I'm sure there are a few eighth generation Vermonters out there who look down their noses at her for being a newcomer, or, as we say up here, a flatlander. I go by the accent, the vocabulary, and the New Hampshire test: if you speak in a clipped, almost honking dialect; if, when thanked for doing something you cackle, "Not a problem!"; if, when someone mentions the state of New Hampshire the bile rises in your throat, then you are a native Vermonter.

There are some family names in Stowe that have been around since the time of the dinosaurs. They are the names that have become part of the land themselves: Percy, Adams, Mayo, Taber. The people who wear those names—and others I've failed to mention—are all real Vermonters. But some of them fall into the category of local business people who depend on tourism to earn a living, and that's the second major division within the town: business people and tourist-residents.

People have always come to live in Stowe because of the skiing, and because of the beauty. Very few people used to come to Stowe for the reason people moved out from the cities and into the suburbs: there's no major metropolis to commute to. Instead, people immigrated to Stowe, leaving everything that they knew behind—until the 90s, when the town began experiencing the effects of the economic boom that gripped the world. The nouveau riche arrived here on ski vacations, took a look around, and decided that they could live here, that they had enough money to either retire early, or run a small, Internet-based business from Stowe. Or they were executives who came with some of the bigger companies that were relocating around Burlington, which was only a 45-minute drive from Stowe.

These people are easy to spot because they're so clean. They look like they shower every twenty minutes. They shave all the time, and they wear clothes that come from a catalogue. They go to one of the local gyms and walk on treadmills next to windows that look out on miles of open land crisscrossed with hiking and biking trails. They smell nice. They drive large vehicles and they wash them often. The women don't work and the men appear not to work.

They don't wear baseball caps, and if they do, they wear one of those bizarre custom Red Sox hats with weird colors that some marketer who also shaves a lot and smells nice thought up. At night they go home and sit around a kitchen island so large it can be seen on Google Earth, and sip chardonnay.

These are the people who complain mightily about the traffic jams on the Mountain Road during busy weekends. I should stop here and describe a typical Stowe traffic jam: sometimes cars are backed up for three minutes on Mountain Road leading to the intersection of routes 108 and 100. It's ghastly.

Even within the business community there are divisions. There are restaurateurs and retailers, professionals and shopkeepers. And of course, there are innkeepers. There's a whole slew of us, and we're a bizarre, eclectic group, impossible to profile. An inn is as expressive of the individuals who run it as are the cars they drive. In fact, vehicles are a great way to highlight the individuality of the innkeepers. Let's start with us.

We drove up to Vermont in a '98 Plymouth Voyager minivan, which we thought was pretty slick at the time. It had 35,000 miles on it, and it reeked of practicality. It was the only car we owned. I drove it to work every morning, leaving Chantal essentially stranded here at the inn. She didn't complain; in fact, she liked having only one vehicle.

It appealed to her sense of conservation. After all, she'd grown up in France, where having even one car was a luxury. But I soon convinced her we needed another vehicle. The boys were getting older, and becoming involved in more activities, and though she was no soccer mom, Chantal did need to have mobility. What we needed was one and a half cars. Instead we bought a pickup truck.

I'm a pickup guy, and always have been. Cars have never interested me. Cars you drive down the street. Maybe take someone for a ride. Pickup trucks with four-wheel drive can go in the woods. You can haul crap around in pickup trucks. The commercial fishing culture I came from was dominated by pickup trucks. All my high school friends had pickup trucks at one time. Kevin Mullaney had a gorgeous Chevy Silverado, midnight blue with silver trim. Jimmy Glynn had a couple of Toyota pickups, the kind with the extra little space behind the seats that you could fill up with empty beer cans. Pete Madden used to drive his father's old Dodge pickup around. They were Dodge people, and they had a powder blue Dodge station wagon that dated to antiquity, which one night ran over my foot. Even Tim Durant's father had a pickup, a Chevy or GMC that was held together with rust.

It's not surprising that the first thing I did after college was buy myself a pickup truck. I had been driving a '77 Chevy Malibu, but by 1986 it had self-destructed a couple of times, and I was making enough money to buy a 1986 Ford F-150, 4X4, charcoal gray, 5-speed, with a hose-out interior. It came with a bench seat and an AM/FM radio and it cost about ten thousand dollars. It was a very cool truck, and I was deeply in love with it. I immediately improved it—I tricked it out, in the lingo of the modern era. I installed a sunroof, some custom floor mats, a bed liner, and wheels: Wrangler Radial tires with Keystone chrome rims. It was an extremely cool looking vehicle, and when my father saw it he said, "That's a real whore wagon." I smiled and thought, "Exactly."

So time marched on, I couldn't take it to France, I sold it, broke my heart, but never got over pickup trucks. My logic for buying another pickup truck after we became innkeepers was this: we needed something to haul crap around in, something to use around town while I was at work for most of the day. It also had to accommodate the entire family. My solution was a '93 Ford F-150 4X4 XLT Lariat Super Cab with a full bed. It was black with red cloth interior, and it actually had a bench in the extra cab section. It was roomy and comfortable to drive, but it was as long as a battleship and it needed a ground crew to turn it. It was only a couple of thousand dollars, and I should never have bought it, because like all used vehicles nearing their tenth birthday, this one turned out to be a pain in the ass.

There was one tire that never held air pressure. It had two gas tanks, one of which leaked and was out of service, a fact I didn't learn until after I bought it and my brother-in-law tried to do me a favor and fill the thing for me, and we ended up catching the run-off with milk jugs. But most of all it had a nasty habit of eating up starters. I became adept at installing starters on the truck, and I can assure you that's not the best way to spend a January evening in Vermont. We owned it for a year and a half, and of course nobody wanted to buy it from us. We ended up selling it at auction for less than we paid, and that cured me of old pickup trucks.

Other innkeepers drive vehicles commensurate with their level of innkeeping. Amy and Hap, who own a luxury place called the Stone Hill Inn, drive one of those fancy crossover vehicles. They also have a nice Chevy pickup truck with a plow, and Hap recently bought himself a Harley-Davidson Road King, which he was born to ride. When our friends Mary and Brien owned the Burgundy Rose Motel, they had a pickup truck and a minivan. And Ken and Barb, who own the Season's Pass across the street—which is a place similar in price to ours—own a slew of vehicles, all of them older. It's yet another thing that distinguishes us from each other.

When we came to Stowe, we joined an organization called the Stowe Area Association. They are the professional organization in town, and they operate much like a chamber of commerce. But since they are a private group with no public affiliation, they act slightly differently. The SAA promotes the local businesses and the Stowe brand itself. They publish a dining guide and generally offer benefits to members that range from health insurance—which, as we've seen, is no real bargain—to a vast social network. It's within the scope of this network that we have found most of our innkeeping friends. Every other month or so, the SAA hosts a mixer—a social event all members are invited to. It's a chance to network, to catch up on things with other business owners, and there's free beer and wine. It's usually the only time the innkeepers get together.

Our innkeeper friends are an eclectic bunch. They come from wildly different backgrounds and are here for wildly different reasons. Let's start with Amy and Hap from The Stone Hill Inn. They came from Virginia, where they had a successful restaurant. They built their inn from the ground up into what is now consistently ranked as one of the top ten luxury B&Bs in the country. On paper we have nothing in common—we cater to the opposite profile: a room at The Stone Hill Inn costs anywhere from $295 to $425 a night. But we get along just fine, almost reveling in each other's challenges. Chantal and I abhor the notion of dealing with people who would pay that kind of money for a room. With that kind of expense comes the expectation of something more, and we just don't fit that profile. Innkeeping at that level wouldn't allow us to be ourselves, and that's not an option for us. I'm not suggesting that Amy and Hap are phony; quite the opposite. They're both well-equipped to handle the profile of their customer. They're adept at separating those people from their money. They're charming and subtle and gracious and they possess an attention to detail that borders on disquieting. But the result is inarguable. The Stone Hill Inn is something that could be framed and hung on the wall of the innkeeping art gallery.

Probably our best friend in the business is no longer in the business. Mary Kamm and her husband Brien owned the Burgundy Rose Motel. We were very much alike both in the profile of guest that stayed with us, as well as our approach to innkeeping: we liked to keep it simple. Mary had worked for Ben & Jerry's before becoming an innkeeper, as a food chemist. That meant that she helped invent some of the most famous ice cream flavors in the world, like Cherry Garcia and Chunky Monkey. But like a lot of people, Mary and Brien dreamed of being on their own, beholden to no man, so they jumped into the Burgundy Rose.

Like us, Brien had to work outside the inn to help with expenses, and this despite the fact that Mary was very successful. In fact, in the first couple of years that we were innkeepers she helped keep us afloat, sending us all her overflow customers. But she wasn't immune to problems, and when she began to have issues with her well water, it sounded an alarm. Her expenses began to rise even as her profits rose, but she couldn't keep pace. They sold the inn after five years and moved to upstate New York.

A lot of our original friends have left the business. Steve and Suzanne Vazzanno, owners of the Three Bears at the Fountain, have gone. The folks who owned the Season's Pass when we first arrived have also gone. The litany of turnovers is too long to go into. One of the reasons people don't last that long as innkeepers (industry average is five to seven years) may be that it's a business that's as easy to get out of as it is to get in to. The major asset of the innkeeping business is the real estate. Most B&Bs can be resold as residential property, making a fast escape by frustrated or burned out innkeepers an option. The people who get trapped are the ones whose businesses can't be sold as residential property, and I'm afraid we fall into that category.

And, of course, there are the tragic innkeeping stories, stories of love and loss, stories with subplots you'd never dream of. One of the venerable old places in town was recently auctioned off. The owner tried to get into the real estate development game and found himself overextended.

The place sold at auction for about half its value, and after something like 18 years those folks were out of the business. Others simply tire of the grind and fold their hands and move on. Some spend their way into oblivion. The past couple of years have been rough on innkeepers and restaurateurs in Stowe. A lot of places are just gone. Inns like the Woodchip, the Seibeness, Two Dog Lodge, Andersen Inn, Blair House Manor, the Scandinavia Inn, Three Bears at the Fountain, and restaurants like Mes Amis, Grill 108, Oliver's, Miguels, and Flavor—all gone, and none replaced. There's a definite tightening going on.

It may be time for us to move on. After eight years, we're definitely looking for new opportunities, new adventures for us and our children. That may or may not include innkeeping. It may or may not involve staying here in the States. But we'll always keep Vermont, the place we thought we'd never be able to live.

Shawn Kerivan

<u>Chapter Twenty-one</u>
Group Efforts

A bed and breakfast that can accommodate a busload of people probably isn't a bed and breakfast. Then again, I'm not in the business of defining what makes a bed and breakfast a bed and breakfast. I've spent eight years as an innkeeper and an entire year writing this book in order to dispel the genteel notions people have about innkeepers and innkeeping. But there's just something incongruous about seeing a gigantic box with wheels roll up in front of something as unique as a bed and breakfast. And anyway, what bed and breakfast has that many rooms? Now you're talking hotel. Now you're talking staff.

The allure of groups is strong for a simple reason: they offer the ability to fill more rooms with less effort. One phone call to a bus operator over the summer can fill a place up for a weekend in the winter, and that's worth more than the price negotiated; that's worth peace of mind, because the bus is going to arrive come hell or high water—or a rainy winter weekend. By then, the money's in the bank, and groups tend to sort themselves out. And if you don't believe me, try dealing with eight individual guest rooms when the January thaw arrives.

But groups remain the domain of the bigger places in town. The Commodores, the Stowe Motel, the Northern Lights—all those places have 40 or more rooms, and they need buses, because they just wouldn't make it without them. That can be a big part of their marketing plan, and they spend hours on the phone trying to line up buses for fall foliage, winter weekends, and summer events. They've got to have them; they have staff to pay.

From our point of view, certain groups looked interesting. A small ski club, for example, with fifteen or twenty members, would be a nice fit up here. A mountain biking club would also be a great fit, especially in the summer. We've tried them, but had no real luck. And I'll admit that our effort was half-hearted. During the first couple of years, when we could have used the business, it seemed like a good idea. But things picked up, and we decided we didn't want to pursue that aggravation. Then something fell in our lap.

Our friends Julian and Kay run a place on the Mountain Road called the Riverside Inn. When we met them, we hit it off instantly. Julian and Kay are English, and they ended up in the States due to Julian's job as an importer. They were skiers as well, and after visiting Vermont they decided to stay in Stowe and buy the Riverside. The Riverside is as eclectic as the Auberge, and that was another thing we had in common. We both approached innkeeping from a pleasurable position. We were in it for the lifestyle, not the potential for profit.

The Riverside is a hybrid. The main building houses the inn, an old place with creaky floors that tilt wildly in spots. The guest rooms are simple, and the bathroom's down the hall. These are their value rooms, which can be had for about fifty to sixty dollars a night, depending on the season. But there's another building, behind the main inn, that has motel units, which nets them more money, and gives them flexibility in what they offer. One thing they don't offer is breakfast, and that is more typical of a classic inn, the kind which is rarely found anymore. But it also offers them a challenge in keeping the rooms booked. With more rooms available, Julian and Kay can solicit groups, and one of the groups they get each year is the Harvard ski club.

According to Julian, it all started when one year some Harvard medical students came up to ski. They had such a great time, and appreciated the value, that they came again. Word spread to the Harvard ski club, which comprises undergraduate students, and the next year they showed up. In a bus. Soon there were two buses, and they'd outgrown Julian's place. But Julian hadn't outgrown their money, so he called us and asked if we'd take the overflow. We demurred. Then he told us how much we'd collect for five nights, and suddenly there was a box with wheels parked in front of our bed and breakfast.

Getting the bus here was the easy part. But Julian warned us that though these were Harvard undergrads, they were still undergrads. He began telling us of the wild parties and occasional destruction that occurred at his place. Even though we've gone to great pains to keep the Auberge un-fancy, the thought of wanton destruction at the hands of drunk college kids wigged us out. And then there was the issue of the food and the kitchen. At Julian's place, they had the run of the place, including the kitchen. That meant they prepared their own meals. Chantal decided that would not be the case when they arrived at the Auberge. When the bus rolled up, she climbed on before anyone could get off.

"Hi, everyone. Welcome to Stowe! It's going to be a great week, we've got tons of snow on the mountain!"

(Cheers, hoots, whistles.)

"We're really pleased to have you staying with us, but we have a few rules that are different from the Riverside."

("Wha?" "Huh?" "Has anyone seen my iPod?")

"We have a hot tub out on the back deck, and you're welcome to use it."

("Owwww!" "Oooh, baby!" "Yeah!" Assorted 70s guitar noises.)

"The hot tub is available from four to ten p.m. And no more than four people at a time, please."

("Group grope!" "I'm wearing my Speedo!" "Where's my fucking iPod?")

"The kitchen is off limits. It's our private space. Please respect that."

(The sound of a lone cricket chirping.)

"We'll prepare breakfast and dinner for you. Breakfast is at 7:30, dinner is at six. We'll leave the lunch meat in the fridge in the breakfast room so that you can make your own sandwiches. Any questions?"

(Murmuring, yawning, stretching.)

"Okay, then come on in, we'll show you around."

("Hey, I found my iPod!)

It was late January, and it was cold. I immediately began to fret over the pipes in room 1, which are partially exposed. Whenever the temperature dips below zero for an extended period of time, they're apt to freeze. Over the years, I've struggled to come up with a solution to the problem. Of course, the solution is to throw a wheelbarrow full of money at it when spring rolls around, but things never seem that bad in May. There've been dark winter nights when I've had to crawl under the house with a flashlight and a blow dryer and try to unfreeze a pipe or drain. Once I borrowed a kerosene blast heater from Steve at Three Bears. That night was well below zero, and while the heater—which looked and sounded like a jet engine—did the job of heating up the space and unfreezing the pipe, I couldn't leave it on overnight, not with a bright orange flame licking out of it. So, a few hours after turning the heater off, the pipe refroze.

The problem lies in the construction of this old place, and the nut job who built the bathroom for Room 1. Obviously an add-on, the bathroom was built over a section of the porch that eventually became the breakfast room. And though that room was enclosed, the underside was open to the outside air, separated only by painted plywood. When the northwest wind kicked up, cold air swirled through that space, penetrating everything, freezing pipes. I've toyed with solutions and Band-Aided the thing repeatedly. Once I put a portable electric heater under there, but that didn't last; the heater conked out, the pipes froze. Finally I moved the water pipes so that they didn't pass outside on their way to the bathroom. Now I have to contend only with the drainpipe for the shower and sink, and the toilet. For the shower and sink I've begun pouring windshield wiper anti-freeze down the drain on the coldest nights, thus preventing freezing. I realize this isn't environmentally sound, but it will have to do until I demolish and rebuild the bathroom. All that was far from my mind when our first Harvard crowd checked in. I was concerned with electricity.

They came with every kind of electric and electronic device imaginable: iPods and laptops, yes, but more: hair dryers and cell phones, speakers for their laptops, and things I couldn't—and didn't want to—identify. And when they came home from skiing, they plugged everything in. Like the plumbing, the electricity on this place is skewed. Circuits don't make any sense. One circuit comprises one plug in our bedroom, Room 7 (except for the air conditioner plug, which is on its own circuit), Room 1, the bathroom in Room 6, and the breakfast room. This is the problem circuit. It's overloaded to begin with, and when college sophomores all plug their hair dryers and curling irons in, it trips. And it did.

The first year the Harvard group stayed with us, our big challenge was managing the food. They came with so much of it, we had to figure out a menu. But things smoothed out quickly when we made a menu: one night was tacos, another was chicken burgers, another was spaghetti, another was pizza. It was more work for us, but it kept everybody happy. By the second year, a rule was established: partiers go to the Riverside; the Auberge was a more mellow scene. Having Harvard kids stay with you has added benefits. One year we had computer problems. My computer wasn't talking to my DSL modem/router, and I was lost trying to fix it. But one young man—who writes software programs in his free time—came into my office and fixed things quickly. He explained what he did, and how I could fix it in the future, but the moment he left all that information evacuated my head.

The third year of the Harvard group was more difficult. There was a budgetary crackdown sweeping the ivied walls in Cambridge, and the ski club arrived for a five-night stay with only one day's worth of provisions. It's supposed to work like this: had the ski club not gone skiing, they would have been on campus anyway, and they all would have been eating in the caf, using their meal plans. The university is supposed to supply them with the food they need for those five days and nights. That means that 75 students times three meals a day, times five days, equals 1,125 meals. But some administrator—undoubtedly a brilliant theorist with no practical knowledge of real life—decided that money could be saved, and screwing the ski club out of their food was a great place to start. They were sent up with one day's worth of food.

There's nothing Chantal likes more than a challenge, and this would do the trick for her. Stretching food and keeping people happy ranks among her favorite activities. But this would test her. There would be nothing to raid from the stores of the Riverside, where the bulk of the food was kept. And we could ill-afford to dole out our own supplies; that wasn't included in the price.

Bread was a big problem, so some of the kids went out and bought some. That solved the lunch problem, because lunch meat and cheese were plentiful. Spaghetti was one meal, and we figured out how to control portions: instead of just cooking everything and putting it out there for them to fight over, we served it in stages. And when it was chicken burger night, we only had 23 burgers for 23 people, with potato chips as a side. Chantal made the announcement that if anyone took more than one, someone would get shafted. By the last night, the food situation was Dickensian. Chantal made a sortie to the Riverside, and came back with ten pounds of mutant carrots the size of baseball bats. From that she whipped up five gallons of carrot soup, which everyone loved, despite the chunks of tofu she tossed in with it.

As much as we look forward to the Harvard crowd arriving, and the subsequent deposit of several thousand dollars into our bank account, we still love to see them go. And while that means peace and quiet—at least for a few days—it also means clean up and damage control. Since we don't do housekeeping during their stay, we fill bags and bags as we pass through the rooms. After three years of doing this, we've never had anything approaching the kind of damage that Julian's dealt with. Bent curtain rods and scuffed walls are as bad as things get for us. After their third visit, however, we had to throw away a couple of mattresses.

When the bus rolled up, I hopped on to give them the pep talk. Most of the kids that were staying with us had been at the Auberge before, and that year they even assigned rooms based on occupancy. It was dreamy. All I had to do was call out a room number, and that group would get out, go in, and our sons, Seamus and Brendan, would show them around to their room. Just before Harvard arrived, Chantal and I had changed the beds in Room 1 from two full-size beds to two queens. We had wanted to put the queens in Room 4—because that room gets rented more than Room 1—but Room 4 wasn't big enough to accommodate two beds that size.

When I called for the Room 1 people to come out first, four dainty young ladies exited the bus and went in to their rooms. I then assigned six people to the two-bedroom suite downstairs, which had a queen and a twin bed in one room, a full and a twin in the other. And when I called for Room 4, four giants—football and rugby studs—stood up and lumbered past me. My first thought was, "Ooopsie." I dashed back into the inn, but the girls had already spread out in Room 1. Oh well, the big guys were just going to have to get along in a room with two full-sized beds. I didn't want to think about it. To their credit, they never complained. But when they left, and Chantal and I went in to clean the room, we paid for our mistake. Both mattresses were collapsed, victims of a nightly dose of 500 pounds of flesh. It looked like someone had taken an ice cream scoop and removed their middles. The troughs that remained could have been filled with water and turned into a wading pool. Fortunately, we had a new mattress in reserve, downstairs, and we were able to change one out right away. Another would come from the full-sized bed in Room 3, when we put bunk beds in there this spring.

For us, the nicest thing about the Harvard group has always been their behavior while staying with us. True, we laid down the law on day one and didn't waver, but they were always respectful and polite. They came, they skied, they left. What more could you ask from a group?

Shawn Kerivan

Chapter Twenty-two
And in the end...

This is the end of the line for this place. I mean this building. It will never be a bed and breakfast the way it is now. There are several reasons why. First, unless someone had enough money to buy this place and run it as a hobby, for shits and giggles, it would never work. The amount of money this place could generate as a B&B wouldn't come close to covering the value of the real estate and accompanying mortgage. And why would someone with that much money choose a funky little roadside inn like this when they could have any place they wanted? Stranger things have happened. And yet...

I don't know if we're ready for it to end. There's something comforting about maintaining this lifestyle. I can hustle and teach at the local colleges, ad infinitum, maybe someday getting a permanent position somewhere. We can scale down or scale up this business as needed, and we'll soon be ten years into a twenty-year mortgage, which is a good feeling. And the value of commercial real estate is only going to climb as this section of the town becomes more and more desirable. That leaves more time for skiing, and more time for us to take real vacations. But we want something more, and I don't mean money.

Our sons, Seamus and Brendan, are both in middle school, and soon they'll be at a critical stage of their education. Both Chantal and I have agreed that they need to be challenged more. While Stowe has a fine school system, we're seeking a different level for the boys, and we'd like that to involve education in France, perhaps. In fact, after ten years back in the States, we're pining for something different. After eight years of watching America being led down the toilet by a de facto emperor, we feel the need to go out in the world and show people that Americans aren't dumb animals. And we don't want our sons to grow up with the narrow views shared by so many others.

This is particularly acute for me. By the time I met Chantal, I was a wreck. I had a desire to be different, but I'd never been able to articulate that desire. I had to leave everything I knew in order to grow. And growth is important for the development of our sons. They need that different view, more than can be provided by simply traveling. They need the experience engrained into them, to become a part of them. Then they can flourish.

Those thoughts have led us to become more active in taking the first steps in what may become our transition away from innkeeping. And we've visited a couple of properties in the last year. The first one was in Wolcott, about 30 minutes northeast of Stowe. It was on 30 acres, and it needed some work, and we weren't too serious about it when we went to look at it, but it got us thinking. It got us shaking the routine from our heads. What if we did buy a piece of property? What would we do with it? And would we sell the inn?

Our initial thought would be to manage the property as a vacation rental. We could link its availability to the powerful Stowe Area Association website, giving it plenty of exposure. And we could also investigate renting it traditionally. So we did a little homework, but we found the numbers weren't to our liking. That meant we probably weren't ready to take that step yet. Later that year, we went to a property auction. We got the information a bit late, and we had to hustle to put something together for the bank, but the property went for more than we were willing to pay for it. This time we were ready to commit, and that surprised us. We didn't realize how motivated we'd become, how ready we were to move on to something new. With respect to the inn, one of Chantal's ideas was to lease it to someone, with an option to buy. That seems to contradict my earlier contention that this place could never be sold as an inn, but offering it as a lease would get someone in here, for a year or two, give them an opportunity to go through a cycle, and decide whether they want to do this. It would also give us some income from the place while affording the potential buyers the chance to build a little of their own potential equity toward the purchase. That would put them in a better, more accessible financial situation when the time came for them to buy. It would also give us time to ease away from this place. And finally, it would guarantee that Stowe didn't lose yet another small, family-run operation. But that may just be wishful thinking on my part.

By the spring of 2008, the Stowe Mountain Lodge, at the base of Spruce Peak, is scheduled to open. While its 372 luxury rooms will be priced significantly higher than those of the Auberge, and while it's opening just as the country heads into a major economic recession, the future of this place is clear. Old-fashioned B&Bs will become ever harder to find, as the genuine is replaced with the contrived. And someday even the Auberge de Stowe will be a memory, and all we'll have of that history is a photograph that makes us realize it's not coming back anymore.[15]

Shawn Kerivan

Appendix
InnSights: The Columns

Author's Note: This selection of my columns from the Stowe Reporter is reproduced here with the blessing of the newspaper. The order of the columns is roughly the order in which they appeared, between June, 2001 and March, 2003.

InnSights: "The Idea Guy"

It was one of those fat Vermont mornings that make you wonder what clocks are for. Dollops of mist hung in lacquered sheets over Cady Hill and the promise of rain, spring rain, soft and cool and sweet, stung the air. These are what I call the coffee commercial times, when I fill my mug, take a deep whiff of bean vapor, and check to see if Juan Valdez is hiding around the next corner.

The inn is half full and I'm worried about the guests in Room One. Three girls from Quebec came down for Stowe's version of a pub-crawl: Margaritas at Miguel's, Rolling

Rocks at the Rusty Nail, and Mudslides at
the Matterhorn. I know because one of them
told me last night at 11:30 when she asked
me to open a bottle of wine for them. By the
time I got back with the corkscrew, she was
snoozing in the lobby. Mid-morning and still
no signs of activity. I just want to make
sure they are out before the charwoman goes
in there (we already ran their credit card).

Outside, above, and all around, work
continues on the venerable old place. The
metal roof has been well received, and now
the water comes off it at breakneck speed.
Which, we hope, will lead to a decrease in
the number of buckets needed to catch the
interior drips. The new decks are getting
nailed together finally. I go out and survey
the quality of the work and think, I could
build these myself if I wanted. I just don't
have the time. I could, you know.

That reminds me: I just refurbished the
boys' room downstairs and I need to deal
with the recurring water problems.
Insidious, calculating, unpredictable, water
finds its way into the basement despite my
best efforts. I'm currently considering a
giant umbrella with the inn's name
emblazoned on it, but I don't think that
will fly with the zoning board.

Then there's the breakfast room, the focal point of every inn. When the inn is full, the competition for the two small tables in front of the windows is keen. Guests, previously unknown to one another, now jockey for table position. To secure prime seating, savvy lodgers will sometimes send a scout ahead. Many mornings we'll arrive to find Englishmen, Dutchmen, and mortified Long Islanders squaring off for prime croissant space. What we need is more window seating….

Speaking of window seating, one of the prime spots to eat breakfast has been embellished. Starlings have built a nest in the eve above one of the window tables. Scratching and frantic chirping emanate from the ceiling from early morning to late evening. I was so concerned about this bothering the guests that I formulated a plan to remove them. But much to my amazement, people just love watching the parent bird fly up with a beak full of worms. They sip their coffee and eat their cantaloupe wedges and it absolutely delights them. OK, OK, the starlings live. But as soon as they move out, I'm cementing shut their nest.

Oh, I've got ideas. Lots of ideas, lots of coffee, and lots of time to watch the mist drift across the river.

InnSights:
"Friday Night at the Fights"

It was a Friday night like any other mid-winter Friday night in the innkeeping business in Stowe: we had all just sat down to dinner, crossed ourselves, thanked the Big Guy, and were about to dig in when…

The phone rang first. Though Thursday nights are usually reserved for endless hours of phone ringing and room booking, there is always a last minute barrage of desperate skiers looking for accommodations. No sooner had my wife dispatched that wave of New Yorkers to their cozy digs than the bell on the front door jingled. Keeping a small inn, I was quickly learning, was akin to some twisted Pavlovian experiment devised to test your tolerance to the jingling of bells. I can only say that it's a good thing bell-wearing cows didn't wander by my door, else we'd be buried in sirloins.

By the time we had made it half way through the meal and my wife still hadn't returned from checking in the guests and showing them to their room, we began to worry. This could only mean one thing: the new arrivals were interesting folks and my wife was chatting them up, which is one of the reasons we got into the innkeeping business in the first place. I went looking for her and found her down in the basement scowling at one of the heaters.

I should explain that in the small basement under the inn there were no less than four different heaters: two for hot water, one forced hot water for heating the rooms, and one to heat the hot tub. Leading to and from these heaters an array of plumbing, a head scratching jungle of copper and cast iron.

"There's no heat in room six," she informed me. "But," she continued, "there is heat in five, two, and three. Nothing in four."

"Who's in six?" I asked.

"Young guys. Traveling with their friends from room five."

"Four?"

"They won't be here till 11 or so."

"What about one?"

"That gets heat from the hot air on the other side of the house."

For a moment my eyes narrowed. Was my wife making an oblong reference to me and my proclivity for pontification? She was inscrutable. I moved on.

"Here's what we do," I said. "Tell the guys in six to spend some quality time with their pals in five. Sell them on the heat in five and the lack thereof in six. Tell them I'm working on it, it'll take me two, three beers tops to figure it out. The people in two and three might experience a slight chilliness. This will be temporary. Might want to give them a heads up. I'll get right on it."

My wife now looked at me dubiously. Would she buy it? She had to. Plumbers were sixty-five bucks an hour in the real world, ninety an hour in Stowe.

Five beers later I was on the phone with the heating company. It was 9:30 p.m. and ninety bucks an hour was starting to look like a bargain. I was missing a hockey game and thus far had succeeded only in knocking out the heat to room two.

The heating company sent Don over, a nice, careful guy who really didn't know what he was up against. He kept asking if he could use the phone so that he could speak with Kevin, whom I assumed knew what Don was up against. About 11 o'clock, after succeeding only in dismembering several circulators, he told me Kevin was coming over.

Great: 180 bucks an hour, no hockey game, and I was out of beer. Kevin finally arrived and told me that they needed to replace a part that they didn't have. What Kevin did, though, was rig a by-pass so that at least all the rooms would have heat overnight. I went up to tell the guys in five that half of them could go back into six, but nobody answered the door. I didn't blame them.

By the time I got to bed it was nearly time to get up and make coffee for the skiers. Thank God for the snow. Just another Friday night at the inn.

InnSights: "The Tao of Skiing"

In this world, there are some things that have a symbiotic relationship, things that just go together: Lennon and McCartney, filet mignon and an '82 Chateau LaFite-Rothschild, Hemingway and adventure. To that list you can add skiing and inns.

By no means is this meant to slight the amenities offered by some of the finer resorts and hotels that are found around world class ski areas like Stowe. Many folks prefer the all-inclusive options, the convenience and choice they offer. But when you stand in the parking lot at the foot of Mt. Mansfield and gaze up at the famous Front Four, the tradition, the oneness, the pure and uncomplicated wildness of the ski experience here invade you.

What does an inn have to offer the powder pilgrims that travel here to pay homage to this spectacular place? Very little, and therein lies the point.

I must confess that skiing is a glue in my life, a common thread that has woven itself throughout, influencing turns and weighing on decisions. It is sinewy and strong and flexible, and it has as much to do with who I am, what I do, and how I got here, as anything else I can think of. I met my wife while we were both ski instructors. We both had a passion for the sport, and skiing has managed to insert itself into our lives right up to our decision to become innkeepers.

The pureness of the skiing spirit has always driven us, has always bound us, and we had a strong vision of what kind of innkeepers we wanted to be. We wanted to have a place that doesn't get in the way of the skier. That doesn't mean that we line'em up on cots in the back hallway and kick'em out before breakfast. What we were searching for was that comfortable, homey feeling. We wanted to partake of that warm, satisfied glow all skiers have as they sit back and remember that near perfect run they had earlier that day.

That spirit has ruled many of our decisions as innkeepers. It has served not only as an identifying marker, but also as an external manifestation of what kind of lodger you'll even consider. That means that sometimes you lose a little business because folks are looking for something a little different. What we've tried to achieve is something that we think closely approximates our shared dreams, something that reflects the great love we have for skiing in

particular, and the outdoors in general. We
can't give people everything; we're far too
small to offer much more than coziness and
ourselves. Today I even talked someone out
of booking several rooms with us. To have
satisfied their needs, we would have needed
three more buildings and far too many hours
in front of the planning commission. They
were looking for something else, and that's
okay. Fortunately there are plenty of great
places in Stowe that had what they were
looking for, and I was able to steer him in
the right direction.

When people come back to us after a day of
skiing, they are absolutely aglow with
excitement. The Mountain has given them all
they need, all that is important to them. We
are there when they come home, we trade
skiing stories and compare all the different
places we've been. Being ourselves as
innkeepers has taken a little practice, but
we've found our niche. This has been fully
evidenced every weekend this winter.

Despite an economy that is supposed to be
on its knees, combined with the
psychological effects of a war, the faithful
are getting in their cars and coming up to
ski. In fact, they're tripping over each
other. The meteorological peculiarities of
this winter—especially coming in the heels

of last year's monster snows—need not be retold. Perhaps a contributing factor to this year's enthusiasm is an echo effect from last year.

What that means for us is not as limiting as it sounds. Far from being simply single season folks, we can't wait to get the mountain bikers, and the hikers, and all the other travelers who love to visit this place. Snow and skiing do not engender a spirit of exclusivity. Rather, they are the reality of a certain combination of things that transcend weather and geography. They are part of a larger spirit, a spirit of humanism that we are so lucky to tap into as innkeepers.

Same as it ever was—and maybe that's the reason. Maybe for skiers all it takes is a great mountain, a little snow, some cold air, and blue skies. Just as innkeepers live for hospitality, so do their lodgers live for that pure, uncomplicated adventure that comes with a ski weekend. As long as they keep coming up the road with that childlike look of excitement across their faces, we'll be here with a place for them to hang their skies and put their feet up.

InnSights: "Got My Mojo Workin'"

At the crossroads of the journey stands the innkeeper. Situated somewhere between the dull edge of twilight and the sharp refrain of dawn, the innkeeper breeches the two worlds of the traveler: the world of the unknown, and the world of the familiar. Offered is the promise of a warm bed. Implied is the prospect of sincere conversation. Given is that, and more. It's got to be the raison d'être of innkeeping, because it sure isn't the money.

It should not be surprising that there is an element of spirituality to this way we have chosen. Not religion; that's too organized for what I mean. Rather, a lightness, a reverence for place and time, an acknowledgment of a higher power. And by higher power I mean that place at the end of Mountain Road, the Mecca that draws the powder pilgrims to our back yard. In the wake of that promise comes the innkeepers, giving the traveler a home and a little bit of time away from their journey so that they may better appreciate, enjoy, and absorb it.

I sometimes refer to this feeling as my innkeeper mojo. Innkeeper mojo is the thing that makes me pull my car over to the side of the road when I see a group of cyclists loaded down with saddle bags on Route 100. Brightly colored, helmeted, bedecked in stretch pants, they're true road warriors. Maps and water bottles occupy the center of their circle as I approach.

True, the first words out of my mouth are, "Do you have a place to stay yet?" But truer still is the spectrum of reasons why I offer them lodging. Their stories surround them like an aura. The easy way their feet grip the road tells me that we are kindred spirits, for what innkeeper isn't also a traveler? We are as interesting as the people we welcome. We know it, but we let the light shine on our guests. It is their moment, and we are happy to share it.

Innkeeper mojo is the thing that comes between other innkeepers when they are sharing. This camaraderie is a very strange thing to become accustomed to, for it seems to contradict logic. But peek under the surface and you'll see it again: the spirit of this place that throws us all uniquely together. Our backyards are mutual and our goals are fairly common. That is why it is not unusual to see innkeepers co-mingling, exchanging ideas—and stories, of course.

Innkeeper mojo is also that thing that rips at me each morning as I drive out of

town. I didn't come up here to leave every
day, I tell myself. I can see it in the
faces of the others that share the road with
me. But that is the way it is, for now.
Besides, when it gets bad during my workday,
I can just look up and see the other side of
the Mountain, and then I feel it all come
back to me. On weekends we see one another
and we understand, because innkeeper mojo
transcends innkeeping, just as spirituality
transcends religion. We laugh and exchange
derogatory tales of commuting and then we
quiet down and watch the sun dip below the
lush green expanse of our lives.

The patron saint of innkeepers is St.
Julian the Hospitaller. His full title is
the patron saint of ferrymen, innkeepers,
and circus performers. It's not surprising
that a medieval Frenchman who relentlessly
battled the Saracens during the Crusades
should have been assigned such a motley
collection to look after. All that traipsing
around gave him ample opportunity to
experience those positioned "along the way."

That position, that station along the
roadside, is what the innkeeper gives. It
cannot be stated as pancakes and sausage, or
a swimming pool, or even a warm welcome. The
innkeeper, much like the writer, transmits.
The innkeeper is a conduit for what this

place is. We can only hope that a small part of that feeling—call it mojo or call it spirit—is passed along. If we accomplish that, we've done our job.

InnSights: "September 11, 2001"

Like many of the columnists here at the Stowe Reporter, I had penned a completely different arrangement of words before the tragic events of September 11, 2001, changed the world. It may have been breezy, it may have been funny, and it may even have contained that germ of Zen insight I feel is so necessary to innkeeping and life. To be truthful, I can't remember, because I haven't looked at it since Draft #1. Right now, things like innkeeper's tales seem brutally inconsequential.

I'm not sure if there is an American among us who wasn't touched by this unspeakable terrorist act. If you weren't affected directly, you'll be affected indirectly. Surely, we all changed, and September 11, 2001, will take its grim place among the pantheon of dates that changed our history, alongside December 7, 1941, and November 22, 1963. Even here, at our small roadside inn, we have felt the echo of the blasts in so many ways.

The most blatant result is cancellations. As of this writing, we have only suffered a few. Two were from visitors who would be flying in to Burlington. They expressed fear not only of potential security breaches, but also of the ability to arrive here on their original schedules, given the instant state of flux our domestic carriers were thrown into. I could sympathize instantly. I work for an airline, albeit one that flies boxes instead of folks, and for two days last week, tens of thousands of us stood idly, bravely smiling, the frustration mounting.

The first time I picked up the phone and had to deal with someone on the other end wishing to cancel, I didn't handle it well. I mumbled, bumbled, and stuttered, and by the time I had hung up the phone, I was awash in a cold sweat, as if a ghost had just visited me. I took a breather and tried to come up with a plan. I figured there'd be more of this ahead of us, and while we would ultimately respect the wishes of people in this difficult time, we also strongly believed that it is of paramount importance to "carry on," as our British brothers say.

The next time someone called up to cancel, I replied, "What can I do to change your mind?" This comment caught this woman off guard, and the result was a long and cathartic conversation. In the end she did cancel her stay, but we both felt so much better for our conversation. We were able to bridge a treacherous gap that has grown instantly within the American psyche, a gap that was the real intent of the gutless terrorists on that Tuesday morning. Just by our mutual expressions of honesty and the connection that resulted, we both felt better. We both felt blessed, and she promised to call back when the dust settled. Whether she does or not is not our focus. We're happy we made a friend, which is why we got into this business in the first place.

The next part of my story deals with the night of Tuesday, September 11, 2001. That day was the eighth anniversary of our marriage, and we had planned a night out featuring dinner at—where else—one of Stowe's incredible eateries. By 9:30 or so that morning, both Chantal and I realized that our plans would be marred. About an hour later we understood that we would never think of that day the same way again. As with other tremendous shocks, the first thing the body does is shut down all sensory perception. We both knew that we couldn't not celebrate our anniversary. Besides, we were both punch drunk from the unbelievable images we had witnessed all day, and the future of my company was anybody's guess at that point. We're still in love, so we went out to eat.

The mood at a candlelit restaurant is always muted, but that night seemed especially melancholy. Looking back, with the benefit of a week's perspective, it was, perhaps, best that we went out that night. The deepness and completeness of the horror had not set in. For a few hours, our little community of Stowe worked its magic on us, and we were able to disengage our brains, if not our hearts. The people eating at the table beside us had a similar experience. After finishing her desert, the woman sitting close to me let out a long sigh, then said, "I didn't think I was going to get through this, but I'm glad we came."

That's when I truly realized how special this place is, and how lucky we all are to live here. Not because we are insulated from the kinds of losses incurred last Tuesday—certainly none of us escaped untouched in some way. But because here at Stowe we live in—and share—such a magical place. Therapeutic is the word that comes to my mind. I'll travel to the Mountain many times in the upcoming days. I'll need its strength. I'll try and tell that to the folks that don't think they can make it up here to visit us. Then I'll let them make their own decisions. And I know that we will all arrive at a better place, because in

Stowe, we're halfway there. God bless
America.

InnSights:
"Sign, Sign, Everywhere a Sign"

I read the news today, oh boy. It wasn't as
bad as it could have been. Nor was it
spectacular. It was…well, it was just about
where we thought it would be. What I'm
talking about is our first year as
innkeepers. We couldn't have imagined a year
in our lives like this past year. Then
again, who could have? Our lives, like our
business, were touched in many ways over the
past year. Many of those experiences have
appeared in this space, and many were just
understood.

Of the many milestones we achieved in our
business, the one that shines above all
others is the day our new sign went up.
Though we had been open and doing business
for some time, we sort of hit the ground
running, without much fanfare or grand
opening galas. Many months before that, when
this had all been a dream, our vision
started to come together. It didn't start
with a name. Instead it began with a notion,
nurtured and slow aged, sampled and added to
over time.

The nurturing part of this dream was years
in the conception. Long development time was

one reason we transitioned into this
lifestyle so quickly and without a lot of
adjustment. We allowed ourselves to chew on
this idea for many years. Those years gave
us time to raise issues, to get comfortable
with the idea, and, if necessary, to bail
out.

The importance of the slow build up cannot
be overstated. When the time came for us to
buy the inn, things happened fast. It's
conceivable that someone could wake up one
morning, fancy being an innkeeper, and a few
months later be greeting people coming
through the front door. The danger in this
is the inherent risk of moving too fast into
the unknown. After all, the difference
between love and flirtation is all the
difference in the world.

The actual naming didn't happen until the
deal was just about done. It reminded me a
bit of naming children. Before you have
children, there is some light talk about
favored names. Some people have it all
chiseled out already. Then, when you are
expecting, the real business of naming the
baby begins. Books are checked out of the
library. Arguments against naming the child
after a long an dead aunt, uncle, or family
pet, are made. There is hashing, and there
is rehashing. Everything is in a name. With

a bit of luck the naming is complete by the time the Happy Day arrives.

The process with naming a business was not dissimilar. We cast about for a while with a list of about 100 names. We argued virtues and accepted limitations. We defined parameters, tried to approach it first from a cold, rational side, then from a purely emotional side. In the end some kind of divine intervention might have played a role, for the name suddenly dawned on us, and the second we heard it, we knew it was right for us. And when the name went up on the new sign on a snowy winter day, it never looked so right.

We didn't get that kind of emotional return from the new metal roof. Oh, it's swell to look at. But it's awfully green and flat, no matter which angle you take. And it went on only piece by piece, so it lacked all the drama of the new name on the new sign. Once on, however, the roof held its own, drawing plenty of compliments. We look forward now to a snowy winter without lots of roof shoveling and strategic bucket placements throughout the inn.

By all accounts we were ready to be innkeepers. By all accounts, no one is ever truly ready for anything. We were baffled by the inconsistencies of July until we found out in November we had been in a recession since March. September was like a gut punch, and not because business was off. November has been a pleasant surprise.

What the past year has done for us is give us fodder. We are armed now with knowledge—albeit only a year's worth—to make a plan. We know better who we are as innkeepers, what we can truly expect from this, and where we want to go with it. And perhaps most importantly, we still have the patience that allowed us to ferment our ideas for so long before acting. We still sit down together and take deep breaths and let it all sink in before talking at night.

Recently, somebody "from away" called us and asked if we still liked it. They wanted to know if we missed what we had left behind. It's almost impossible to answer that because we didn't leave anything behind. Instead we embraced—and were embraced by—a whole new experience in a very special place. Yeah, we still like it. In fact, we love it.

InnSights:
"The Remains of The Stay"

Bo Diddley once sang that "You can't judge the sugar/by looking at the cane/You can't judge a woman/by looking at her man/You can't judge a sister/by looking at her brother/You can't judge a book/by looking at its cover." I'm starting to wonder if old Bo didn't know a little something about the innkeeping business.

It is a natural function of this occupation that you enter into the private space of people with the intention of making beds, reloading The Famous Paper, and straightening up a bit. There is a trust built in to a lodging arrangement, tradition born of civilization, and one that we honor. But after you've tripped over bottles of scotch and had your departing guests leave you tips in the form of melted Ben & Jerry's ice cream, you start to see a real dichotomy that is the human condition.

We had a family staying with us consisting of two doctors and two very intelligent, well-spoken, well-mannered adolescent children. They hailed from Greater Gotham, and that's all the detail I'll provide. As far as guests go, they were easy to deal with. Happy to be here, thrilled with breakfast—especially the bottomless bowls of Raisin Bran—and out on the slopes all day. But when my wife and mother-in-law came down from cleaning the rooms, they wore looks of astonishment.

"Somebody expire?" I asked indelicately.

"Not yet," said my wife. "The family of doctors in the suite? Three bottles of Metamucil on the dresser."

"And," added Trudy, "they were all out of The Famous Paper." She raised her eyebrows and pushed her lips together the way only a mother can.

But that wasn't all. Next to the lifetime supply of Metamucil was a Costco-sized jar of Immodium AD. And these people were doctors. Educated. Intelligent. Thinking of the plumbing battles that must have raged through them made me shudder.

On a more prosaic note, the consensus about what gets left behind by lodgers most often seems to be single socks. We can stop blaming dryers for all the sock theft in the world. Hotels, motels, and inns are littered with single socks. If ever an army of cold-footed, one-legged aliens invades, we'll be able to outfit them.

My personal favorite left-behind item is beers. People love leaving beers. It's a function of the vacation mentality, as in, "We're on vacation, so we must be able to drink lots more, and without regret." Usually they are done in by one of the Mountain Road rehydration spots, and can't face another beer by Sunday morning—never mind dragging them home. They donate them to me by leaving them on their dresser after checkout. If I'm lucky I'll score a growler of Mountain Ale from the Shed. People invariably buy two jugs and pass out before finishing the second, hence the warning, "No drinking in the hot tub." Stop by for a visit on Sunday afternoons when my magic beer fridge is brimming.

Most fascinating about this phenomenon is that they do it consciously, for they must know we'll find what's left behind. It's like a secret code that they use to communicate with us: 2 Coronas, 1 wool sock, a bra, and half a roll of Tums means we had a blast. However, when they leave behind their little pillow gift, you'll never see them again.

And then there are the people that are totally unpredictable, like the two guys in a chimney sweep's van. They were on a ski tour of the northeast, hitting every major area in two weeks. And when they showed up, they were very…out of it. A pungent cloud of happy smoke hung around them; I hesitated before showing them to their room. They looked harmless and happy, and I didn't see any buckets of Metamucil sticking out of their bags, so I figured the pipes would be safe. Then they started asking where the closest pizza joint was, so I settled for reminding them that there was no smoking in the room and telling them that breakfast was at 7:00.

That night, after dinner I looked out the window to see the same two guys standing outside in the snow next to their van. More curious than anything else, I went out to chat them up, and to remind them that the penalties for possessing a Class B substance were pretty much uniform throughout this Great Land.

They were cooking out. They had a small Hibachi set up with a couple of nice looking steaks sizzling, and despite the snowflakes and swirling wind, these two guys were tailgating on a Thursday night in the Lower Village. They had a boom box set politely low—Reggae, of course—and they cradled a couple of cans of beer discreetly while their dinner cooked. I left them to their camping, thinking of what I would tell Stowe's finest, should the need arise.

After they checked out, I ran to their room ahead of my wife—I hadn't told her about their smoky arrival. Alas, I was disappointed. Not only did I not find the place littered with rolling papers and empty bourbon bottles, these guys had even made their own beds. The room was neat as a pin. And they had hardly used any of The Famous Paper. What more could you ask for in a paying guest?

InnSights:
"Should They Stay
or Should They Go?"

There comes a time in every innkeeper's tenure when someone—a close relative, a distant cousin, an estranged spouse—shows up on your doorstep expecting lodging for nothing and their breakfast for free. When you set up shop in a place as lovely and alluring as Stowe, it's inevitable. Like all things in life—and here I'm thinking of the half-hour sitcom—these occasions usually stem from a basic misunderstanding, a failure to communicate.

Zooming out for a moment, we see that this problem is endemic not only to the innkeeper, but to all small business people. The attorney who hangs out a shingle soon discovers the hidden legal problems of friends and family. The butcher is surprised to find out just how many vegetarians will come out of the closet for a pound of really nice German bologna. And, of course, the masseuse who studies all those years to achieve just the right touch finds out how many aching backs dangle from the family tree.

Innkeeping is not immune from this affliction. In many ways, the innkeeper suffers more than other entrepreneurs, because the job of an innkeeper, by definition, is to give so much of oneself, to give so much intrinsic value, that when discounts—familial and otherwise—are expected, the stress of the internal dissension can be monumental. The obvious answer is to adopt a hard line, to take the cue from our nationally historical isolationist past and to adopt a one-price policy: you stay, you pay.

Here's the problem with that solution: we just can't do it. We love meeting and greeting people. We welcome them into our home, for crying out loud. We don't punch a clock. No matter how irritated I am when someone drags me out of bed in the middle of the night, I'm always gracious as I explain that no, I don't have any champagne iced down, and by the way, it's 2:30 in the morning. When we start talking about family, we get all mushy.

Add familiarity to that equation, and things become muddled. After much consternation and observation, discussion and meditation, I think I've reached a middle ground. Anyone with opposing or differing views, ideas, or intuitions are

encouraged to share them. Here's the deal:
your mom stays for free. Everything else is
negotiable.

Let's talk about family and mom. First, a
definition. I suggest a list. Sit down with
your spouse/partner/innkeeping advisor and
define who is and who isn't family. When the
smoke clears, take a deep breath and hash
out a final list. These are the people who
stay for free no matter what. If the bank
forecloses on their house Christmas week,
you set up cots for them in the living room.
If a fire ravages their pad right before the
Antique Car Show, tents pop up on your
property. These are the people you go to the
wall for.

Try and keep this list short. So far, only
my mother, my father, and long deceased
members of my family have qualified for this
list. By long deceased I mean people that
never saw the light of the 20th century.
This eliminates many gray areas and possible
conflicts, such as Great Uncle Wilbur, who
survived a power outage in the hospital. For
a guideline, try the following: only people
who gave birth to you, and people who
cleaned up after you regularly as a child,
should be allowed this accreditation, which
I call Level 1 Status. This status is
accorded the people who really loved you

because they had no choice. As a child you were awful and you smelled badly, but they believed in you and loved you anyway. People like these deserve the red carpet, ad infinitum. Put them in the nice suite whenever possible.

Level 2 Status goes to brothers and sisters and hockey buddies from college. The theory behind this is that these are the people who love you up to a point, that point being anything that might land them in jail. They're true, but not maniacal. Level 2 Status means that during Christmas week, February vacation, and the entire month of August, you're full, no matter when they call. If these people insist on being up here during one of these peak times, refer them to a major hotel chain or campground.

Finally, we come to Level 3 Status. These are the people that I call the Knots, because they seem to come out of the woodwork when you apply the stain. Where were they when I was painting the inn? When these people call, you'll hear things like, "You remember me…I was that guy that sat behind you in study hall in eighth grade…." These folks get a discount on the mud-season price, but that's it. In other words, nothin' from nothin' leaves nothin'.

The inherent problem with the above guidelines is this: there is always a time when your mom wants to come up when the inn is full. No matter how strict you are, or how motivated you are by the goals of your endeavor as an innkeeper, you are going to have to make that tough decision. And when you are trading income for family, just remember this: there is a direct correlation between face wiping and free rooms during August. Your mother said so.

InnSights: "Horse Latitudes"

As the last leaf reluctantly surrenders its final bit of unearthly luminescence, and the hordes recede slowly down the interstate in search of something to carry them through the gray urban winter, we can all unclench those perma-smiles, loosen our belts a notch, and enjoy the bounty. Though we are fortunate to live in a place whose natural beauty sustains us for most months out of the year, seasons inevitably change, and there are a few selected months when everything gears down. In the innkeeping business, these breaks in the action are euphemistically referred to as "value season." In my personal lexicon, I refer to this down time as the Horse Latitudes.

The times I'm thinking of run generally from the end of October through Christmas, and then from sugaring season to somewhere around the middle of May. Like astronauts emerging from their re-acclimation chambers after a long flight in space, during these times we find ourselves gasping with the renewed sensation of gravity. Then realization spreads, and we see the time as a transition that must be endured until the next wave breaks.

These "transition months" offer us opportunity to reflect, to recharge our batteries, and most of all, to panic. Just as we panic when hungry/thirsty/exhausted travelers arrive on our doorsteps en masse, so too do we find ourselves twitching with bewilderment as the Horse Latitudes drag on. What to do?

One of the more popular pastimes is hiring a carpenter to tackle an impossible renovation around the old place. By impossible renovation I mean an improvement that involves renting a crane, or pouring a concrete foundation. Something, in other words, that will require a professional to separate you from your money. By my calculations, there are a total of three carpenters between the Connecticut River Valley and Lake Champlain, and two of them have retired to the small Pacific atolls they bought, grace a nous. So great is the demand for these tradesmen that should you be lucky enough to secure the services of one of them, you will most likely find yourself sharing him with someone else. During the lulls in the seasonal action around here, we all have the same bright idea: Let's add a deck/wing/widow's walk to the place!

If you wait until the last minute to begin
a major construction project, the
aforementioned panic blooms exponentially.
Of course, tardiness in the decision-making
department can be overcome by waving gobs of
money around. But be warned: that approach
risks impugning quality, as contractors try
to serve us all by doubling up on jobs. It's
advisable to have your builder firmly
committed well before the last tracks are
cut into Mt. Mansfield, or before Stowe is
transformed into Little Bavaria. If you're
adding a new roof to the place, for example,
you'll want work to begin soon enough to
warrant the shoveling of snow off the old
roof. That way you can feel good about
seeing the project finished before the
summer crowds arrive.

Having the opportunity to get together
with other innkeepers during thumb-twiddling
season confirmed our suspicions: we were all
trying to get our projects completed during
the lull, and we were all sharing the same
builder. This imparted a new twist to our
coexistence, creating a polite tension that
hadn't been there before. While many of the
inns around Stowe are sufficiently unique as
to preclude direct competition, as soon as
remodeling season kicks in, all bets are
off.

We saw the doldrums as a two-pronged problem: we needed major work done around the inn. This would be pricey, we knew, which led to the second part of the problem: how could we defray the cost of this work while still getting heads-in-beds?

My brilliant solution is to organize workshops and have all the participants stay here at the inn. How would that get the work done, you ask? That's the brilliant part. The workshops will literally be workshops, featuring power tools, paint brushes, and pressure treated lumber. The name of the seminar will be "Fixing Up An Old Inn." Full Continental breakfast included. With yours truly as foreman and chief animator, the program will stress meeting deadlines, coming in under budget, and attention to detail in all phases of carpentry, electrical wiring, and that old standby of ancient inns, plumbing. Call now for availability.

By the way, for those who don't know, the Horse Latitudes is an area of the Atlantic Ocean between 30 and 35 degrees of latitude that features high barometric pressure and little wind. Early European mariners would be tooling along on their way to the New World when suddenly they would find themselves becalmed. In an effort to overcome their lack of forward progress and avoid a mutiny, they would jettison ballast, including horses. While I haven't seen anyone around here forcing horses out onto the street, the principle holds true that during slowdowns you have to be forward thinking,

For now that seems tolerable. Given the level of congenital traffic failure we experience every autumn, the calm is much appreciated. But the wise ones are already waking up to the sound of hammers rapping and diesels idling. The leaves may be the only things falling now, but the skies will soon be blanched with the white stuff, and nobody really wants to look at unfinished projects at Christmas, do they?

InnSights:
"Idiot Boxes…
and Other Tools of the Trade"

TV, or not TV, that is the question: Whether 'tis nobler in the mind to suffer the slings and arrows of the cell phone generation, or to take arms against a sea of satellite dishes and wires, and, by opposing, lose business. To cable TV, to wire rooms with phones—who knows what to do?

While I'm sure the Bard never dreamed his prose would be co-opted to express the frustrations of so pedestrian a pursuit as innkeeping, so too am I sure that he was never confronted with the Byzantine choices innkeepers face when it comes to choosing which technologies you wish to include in your establishment for the convenience and comfort of your guests: Cream or sugar? Oatmeal or eggs? Color cable television or a chair out on the back deck?

Small innkeepers approach the television question with a wide range of emotions, from trepidation to ambivalence to animosity. Because so much of what you do in this métier is a reflection of your personal philosophy, you can't hide your decisions. What you put into your inn says not only

what kind of person you are, but what kind
of traveler you cater to. With that in mind,
we beg the television question.

Though considered still a babe by the
standards of the grizzled and savvy veterans
of innkeeping in these parts, our inn has
already confronted the heinous television
question enough for me to wince at the mere
mention of the word. What we have decided is
that cable television in the rooms is viewed
by the gentle traveler in the same light as
the pool and air-conditioning: you need to
have it on the sign out front to get them in
the door, but once they are here, they could
care less about any of it. In fact, I'm
thinking of replacing our pool with a giant
picture of a pool that I can unroll out on
the back lawn whenever someone pulls in the
driveway.

With the electronic arrival of the
Olympics these past two weeks, the question
has again come to the fore. Last week we had
to break the news to some stunned
snowmobilers that the tiny black and white
telly in their room only picked up one and a
half channels, neither of which televised
the commercials that squash network coverage
of the Olympics, nor the Games themselves.
Luckily they were amenable to viewing the
Games at one of our town's pubs. But the

situation got me going again on the cable
television question.

In the name of research I called an
innkeeper friend who has satellite
television. The response I got, while
refreshing, was eye opening. Apparently, the
TV question is a no-win situation. I was
told tales of customers unfulfilled by their
cathode ray offerings. If ESPN was offered,
someone would undoubtedly complain that they
didn't carry ESPN2. And here's the real
kicker: the satellite system doesn't offer
the network that carries the Olympics, so
we're not alone in our stock of customers
wanting biathlon with breakfast, hockey in
the hot tub, and figure skating by the fire.

What it comes down to is this: Who are
you? What do you want? I've used this space
to say this before, and I'll say it again,
we really love this thing called innkeeping,
and we do it because of the people. And the
kind of folks that stay with us share more
than a love of all the beauty that Stowe has
to offer. They are willing to risk a little
bit of themselves, just at we are, in the
hopes that they will take away something
that you can't save on film. Part of that is
this place, and its dinky black and white
televisions.

When I was a boy, my parents used to take my brother and me up to Twin Mountain, New Hampshire, snowmobiling. As big a thrill as that was, the most fun we had was late at night, watching the tiny black and white television that came with the cabin. We would stay up just to watch the late local news, listening to the newscasters talk about all those northern New Hampshire things that sounded as exotic as Ecuador to us.

There's still a little bit of that in those old black and white televisions we have in our rooms. I like to imagine somebody sitting in Room 2 on the edge of the bed trying to tune in Channel 22 so they can get the late weather report. I imagine them bathed in the fuzzy gray light, squinting, cursing in sotto voce, cajoling the set, holding the antenna at just the right declination, until the weatherman comes into focus long enough to utter that magical word: "Snow."

I can't sell that kind of experience on our Website. Nor can I hang it on the sign out front (all my square inches are used up). I can only hope that when I book a room and that question arises, maybe they'll remember why they chose a cozy little inn in the first place. And maybe when they get here, they'll take one look around and forget.

InnSights: "Tire Kickers"

There are many businesses which invite browsing. These businesses, most of them of the retail variety, have many different items for sale, and browsing is actually part of the selling strategy. The idea is to get the shopper in the front door for one thing, then let them discover many other things to buy once they are inside. Many endeavors are launched on this theory. Innkeeping is not one of them.

Before exploring this phenomenon, I'd like to set it up a little with some comparative background. Like the old George Carlin comedy routine about the differences between baseball and football being so radical, so too does there seem to be a wild dichotomy between winter visitors and summer visitors to our region. It can be like night and day.

When the snow flies, winter people lock and load. They set their sights north, they pack up, and they drive. Their approach to their activity is direct and involves very little of what can be called leisure. The execution of their plans begins on Thursday night, when innkeepers are solicited by telephone for room availability. Skis are strapped to car roofs, woollies are folded into suitcases, and I-89 is filled with powder pilgrims on Friday nights.

These folks are up early on Saturday mornings looking for breakfast. I've often found them wandering around as early as 6 a.m., just staring out at the snow. They take coffee, muffins, croissants, as many carbohydrates as you can give them, then they are out the door, robust and bright eyed and smiling. They are the manifestation of energy in the human body. By five they are back in the hot tub, but not to unwind, for now they are formulating plans for dinner. Everything with winter people is calculated, planned, direct. They are a football coach's dream.

The summer traveler suffers from no such restrictions. Summer people are generated from a more languid place, and are blessed with a more languid pace. They are usually not restricted to any one activity when they arrive here, and they have more time than a weekend to do what they want to do. Summer visitors have blurred their boundaries, loosened any constraints, and put on their sandals. You see a lot of toes in the summer up here.

With the shackles of conformity lying in a smoking heap, the summer traveler drifts more than drives. There's a vast peripheral intake they possess that is missing from winter folk. Their field of view is enormous, their urge browse is insatiable. For retailers, this is a boon. For innkeepers, this can be frustrating.

Here's how the scenario plays out: a car pulls up on a Tuesday evening, usually in the middle of dinner. No one gets out. Two figures can be seen inside, engaged in obvious discussion. Finally, someone exits the vehicle: sometimes it's a man, sometimes a woman; sometimes it's the driver, sometimes the passenger. They enter the lobby: wide-eyed. Do we have a room available? Private bath? What are your rates? May I see the room? Several rooms are shown, emphasis is placed on the property and the view and the pool and the comfort of the rooms. There is polite grunting, thoughtful mmmm-hmmming. Then comes the inn browser's inevitable line: "I have to go speak to my wife/husband/life partner."

The looker, the person who actually comes in to see the rooms, is usually happy with what they've seen and the value of the place. They become your pro forma sales representative when they go out to talk to the person that did not come in, for it is that person that is holding things up. Sometimes they come back in and book a room.

Sometimes there is gesticulating by your sales rep, animated discussion out in the parking lot, fingers run through hair. Then they take off.

In the trade, these people are identified as tire kickers. We've been trying to find a way to prevent this from happening on any kind of a regular basis. One idea is to actually charge a fee for showing prospective lodgers the rooms. Sort of like a mini sightseeing tour, an intra-inn showing charge. Another idea is to actually require any and all persons interested in renting a room to come in and view it—no hanging back shyly in the car while honing your veto power.

It's a summer phenomenon that thankfully doesn't occur all that often. But those are the things you end up obsessing over. Why did they leave? What could I have done differently? That angst is quickly replaced when that other kind of traveler shows up. Those are the folks that come in off the road dog-tired, go for a dip in the pool, and retire for the evening. They're also the ones who are easy to forget, because they're too easy to remember. Besides, they're probably skiers.

Innsights:
The Terroir of Innkeeping

In France, "terroir" is a big deal. Terroir describes everything about the particular area in which a vineyard is located: the microclimate, the topography, orientation, and the soil itself. So focused on terroir are some people that grape variety is almost an afterthought. Recent local mechanical events ignited this French memory of mine.

As we pilot this inn through the swells and swales of one season and another, a certain philosophy emerges, asserting itself the same way that terroir defines the kind of wine that can be produced in a certain area. So absolute is the power of terroir that the same grapes grown under similar conditions in other parts of the world yield startlingly different wines. The same truth holds for innkeepers.

The philosophy I speak about is the feeling we as innkeepers get in this place at this time doing this thing. I have accepted that there will be triumphs and tragedies, and I do so while keeping my specific sight focused on the horizon, and my peripheral sight focused on everything else. It's the kind of stoicism that keeps

the decks steady underfoot. Unfortunately, a
rash of mechanical frustrations has
conspired to colorize my vocabulary and test
my ratchet memory.

Last weekend, amidst an inn full of
guests, the oven gasped its last breath when
the door refused to close. That meant that
in order to bake bread we either had to find
another stove, or raise the temperature of
the kitchen to 400 degrees. Luckily, both my
father and my brother were visiting, and
when it comes to fixing, they shame me.
Alas, no matter how long the three of us lay
on the kitchen floor grunting and poking, we
could not fix that door. We resigned
ourselves to cooking al fresco—gas grill and
open pit—until we could decide the stove's
fate. That was just the beginning of the
trials.

As days lengthen, so does grass, turning a
young man's thoughts lightly to those of
mowing. Modern mowing is achieved in three
stages: riding tractor, for the multiple
acres; push mower, for the crucial front
lawn; and power trimmer, for that fresh
barbered look. Since the front lawn is what
everybody sees, I decided to disinter the
push mower.

I won't lie and say I didn't know the
flywheel on the push mower was kaput. It

happened last September, at the end of
mowing season, and I remember clearly my
reaction then: I'll fix this thing in the
spring. So last week found me diligently
applying my talents in the field of small
engine repair. Here's where philosophy comes
in.

I have no talent for small engine repair.
But, I reason, a mower is a small mechanical
device that was logically designed to
accomplish certain things, notably, spin a
sharp blade two inches off the ground. I
also reason that I am intelligent and
thoughtful, and by applying my calm logic to
the problem of the mower, I would achieve
Briggs&Stratton nirvana. I quickly removed
the flywheel housing, wrapped the new pull
cord, replaced everything, and attempted to
start the mower.

That's when I remembered I had only ten
percent of my right arm to work with. So I
called Chantal, and she tried to start the
mower, but succeeded only in straining her
rotator cuff. Shelving that problem, I
turned to the riding mower. It could be
pressed into service up front and combined
with the trimmer to achieve grassy
presentability. But when I turned the key in
the ignition, a dead battery foiled my
philosophy and me once again. True, the

battery could be jump-started, but that was
not possible right away. I turned to the
trimmer.

Our gas powered trimmer is a beauty, and
it has a certain something that neither of
the other two small engines had going for
it, something I was counting on to save the
philosophical day for me: newness. It was
less than a year old and still shiny and as
I added fuel I hoped it would reward me with
the ear splitting sound of a two-stroke
music. I primed the fuel into the engine,
laid the beast on the ground and braced it
with my right foot, and with my left hand
yanked the starter cord.

On the third tug the trimmer buzzed to
life with its distinctive, high-pitched
drone. I picked it up quickly and regulated
the throttle. Then I raised it triumphantly
over my head, dancing a jig (or maybe it was
a reel) and shouting "Wooo hooo!" I waved to
Chantal and pranced around, annihilating
anything green that had the misfortune of
appearing before me. When I had adequately
marred the yard, I calmed down and reflected
on this small victory. My terroir and my
philosophy were seamlessly blending into
one, and it felt pretty good.

InnSights: "Boom and Echo"

The news rolled in off the wires this week to no one's surprise: the winter of 2001/2002 has officially been deemed the warmest ever—or at least the warmest in the six score or so years that records have been kept. Most folks in these parts knew that without having to be told. We could tell by the height—or lack thereof—of the snowbanks alongside the roads. There are, however, two striking things about this unusual winter. The first is that despite the utter lack of even a single noteworthy snowstorm, we have maintained a decent covering of white throughout the winter. The second is that for the most part, the inn business, at least on a small level, has been brisk.

I'll tell you right up front that my methods for determining how well the small inns around town are doing is crude and voyeuristic. It consists of me driving around town and seeing how full everyone else's parking lot is. Seeing scads of cars bearing Connecticut license plates in every driveway but my own is enough to induce a bi-polar fit of marketing and self-doubt: What are we doing wrong? How did they get a full house in late April? Should we consider skywriting over the Jersey shore as a viable form of advertising?

Actually, there is enough interface and panicked Friday night phone calls between most of us innkeepers to accurately gauge how we are collectively doing. And this winter, there have been a lot of full parking lots. Certainly one reason is that unlike our neighbors in the southern part of the state, we have had the above mentioned snow cover, keeping us in ski conditions that varied from decent to very good throughout most of the winter. Old Mt. Mansfield seems to be able to whip up enough natural snow mojo to give us a white winter. But I think that there are a couple of other factors at work here.

The first is what I call the "Echo Effect." Whenever there is a boom, it is followed by an echo. Last winter was the boom. This winter is the echo. So fabled has last winter become that it has taken its place among the pantheon of monster winters. And not only was last year a big snow year up here, but up and down the East Coast as well. The backyard syndrome sold a lot of skis and snowboards from Boston to Philadelphia, and it lodged itself in the collective memories of a lot of people. And since everyone had such fun skiing on their new shaped skis last year, they just had to come back up this year, even if their own backyards looked like burnt toast.

This year's echo may have also received an unintended boost from the tragic events of last September. While the travel industry—and the economy as a whole—took a staggering hit in the weeks immediately following 9/11, the trend for many innkeepers in the Northeast has been an intensifying of regional travel. Let's put it this way: if you can get in your car and drive there in less than half a day, folks have been going. From Montreal to Ottawa, from Philly to Providence, many people have rethought their vacation destinations and decided to stay regional.

How else can I explain the happy hoards who waited out a Sunday morning rainstorm to get up on the slopes? As this past weekend approached and the weather forecast became glumly evident, I broke a little sweat on my brow. I imagined seething skiers brandishing soggy lift tickets and decrying that they couldn't even sit in the hot tub because it was raining too hard. And though we couldn't stand the weather, it was about as good as we could have hoped for: sunny spring conditions on Saturday, rain overnight, and clearing conditions on Sunday.

I'm sure there are some who aren't upset to see winter close up shop early. I'm not one of them. Professional concerns aside, a premature end to winter only means an extended mud season, and even I haven't been able to market mud season to gentle travelers. I'm sure there's some sport to be had watching overstuffed SUV's sliding sideways through the quagmire that is River Road, but the gang that stays with us drives those things, so they might not get the humor.

My grandfather used to laugh about the weather and say he never worried about it because there is nothing you can do about it. If it snows, you shovel. If it rains, you pump the water out of your basement. If it's hot, drink a cold beer. He would have made a good innkeeper. His advice frees us to worry about the things we can control, and that is ultimately what keeps them coming up, even when the weather won't cooperate.

InnSights: "Living the Dream"

Sometimes our life perspective is achieved only through the triangulation of travel itself. I suppose it is what a lot of summer folks are looking for when they throw the game plan out the window and just head north with nothing more than a map and the memory of a little place they stayed at years ago. The realignment that they seek comes from viewing themselves from a different angle. It can be therapeutic or cathartic, revelatory or confusing. Innkeepers are not immune from it, either.

The event around which I orbited last weekend was my 20th high school reunion. For me it would be the first reunion I attended, having been ex patria for the others. These things, as many of you will attest, tend to take on a life of their own as the date approaches, and on the ride down to the town of my matriculation I was trying to devise ways to couch what it is I really do.

Armed with the evidence of my past—reprints of published stories and articles, brochures from the inn, pictures of the family, receipts, a well stamped passport—I bravely stepped back in time to the crucible of my adulthood. What happened was not unexpected, but nice anyway. I can now safely say that running an inn is not a real mainstream thing to do. Turns out that it's also what a lot of the people I grew up with would like to be doing: "It's always been my dream to do that." Of course I tried to dissuade them.

It's not the competition I fear. Rather it was out of a sense duty to old friends that I framed my ebullient assessment of innkeeping with the harsh realities of the job. For example, many people were blissfully unaware that room had to be cleaned between guests. When that was explained away with the wave of a hand, I gave more details.

"No, you don't understand," I said. "You have to clean everything. And one of the subsets of everything is the toilet. Think about it." Thoughtful gazes turned sour as personal experiences were grafted onto potential duties while I nodded and emphatically raised my eyebrows.

Most of the time that was enough to cause pause, but if it wasn't, I could call upon a plethora of perplexities: basic wiring, roof shoveling, dinner time tire kickers, high maintenance guests, water and gravity, the phone, plumbing, plumbing, plumbing. When I thought I had gone far enough, I switched gears to dreamy and began waxing rhapsodic about the quality of life that all of us, not just the innkeepers, enjoy up here, which usually lead to one of the great innkeeping paradoxes.

While dropping off some film for developing the other day I saw a friend in the parking lot. We got to talking about vacations and about how all you have to do when you live in Stowe is open up your back door and you are on vacation. It was a subject that came up during the reunion, and to a certain extent it is true. The reality, however, is slightly different, and that's where the paradox is born.

As innkeepers we continually sing the virtues of this place and time. It's tune written long before we came, and one certain to be chorused long after we are gone. Through it all the land will endure. That spirit of transience was what I tried to convey to my old friends last weekend. Just as the traveler passes through our lives in 24 hour intervals, so too do we pass through the time of this geography and meteorology, renting a tiny fraction of its final reality. Sometimes that thought was clouded by beer and smoke and pleasant confab. But sometimes I would find someone staring intensely out across the harbor as I spoke, their reality briefly suspended by an old friend who deigned to change their perspective.

I don't yearn to trade places with anyone. And to paraphrase an old fishing idiom, the worse day in Stowe is still better than the best day almost anywhere else. But the nature of the business is almost defined as passing, in one direction or another. I was pleased to have achieved a certain measure of uniqueness among so many wildly creative and successfully unique classmates. To my amazement, nobody seemed really surprised by my news, which says a lot about how well my friends knew me, and maybe how little I knew myself.

With my outlook freshly re-minted I returned home, exhausted and talked out, but with enthusiasm and peace freely mingling. Though it was not a crisis of faith that gave me new views on what we do, the results were similar. So if you see me humming away while buying up all the drain cleaner, you might attribute it to the recent sale of a manuscript, or a large booking for a critical weekend at the inn. Or you just might remember that sometimes we all need a little adjustment of the focal plane to realize that we're on the right track.

Shawn Kerivan

Acknowledgements

Books don't spring to life on their own, and no one builds them alone. A writer humbly and wearily nods in thanks to those who enabled his task, and I'm no different. This project was many years in the making, and without the encouragement of my wife, Chantal, it would not have happened. I must also thank the Stowe Reporter for giving me a voice as an innkeeper, and the great, nurturing professional community of Stowe and the Stowe Area Association. Much thanks to the editorial board and staff of The Vermont Press for their work and ideas. Thanks to cover artist Taylor James for his excellent work. And thank you to Irish poet James Sheils for being in the right place at the right time. Sláinte!

Notes

1 Davies, et al. *So ~ You Want to be an Innkeeper,* p. 79.

2 Eliot, T.S. *The Waste Land, and Other Poems.* New York: Harvest/ HBJ; 1934.

3 Flaubert, Gustave. *Three Tales.* New York: Alfred A. Knopf, 1924. Pp. 75-121.

4 Stowe Area Association. "History of Stowe, Vermont." *GoStowe.Com.*.<http://www.gostowe.com/about/history.php>

5 Kerivan, Shawn. "Inn Sights: The Wonderful View From My Window." <u>Stowe Reporter</u> 7 June 2001: 14B.

6 National Public Radio. *All Things Considered.* http://www.npr.org/templates/story/ story.php?storyId=18187774. January 17, 2008.

7 http://www.aubergedestowe.com

8 Frey, Evelyn Wermer. "Stowe Writer-Innkeeper to Speak at Library." <u>Stowe Reporter</u>, 1 November 2007: Scene 3.

9 Frey, Evelyn Wermer. "Stories explore hard lives." <u>Stowe Reporter</u>, 1 November 2007: Scene 3.

10 Ibid.

11 http://www.fedex.com/us/about/today/history/

[12] Reiner, Leif Wellington Haase and Cari. "Employer-Based Insurance Leaves Many Uninsured." At Issue: Does the United States Need a National Health Insurance Policy?. Ed. Nancy Harris. San Diego: Greenhaven Press, 2006. Opposing Viewpoints Resource Center. Thomson Gale. Hartness Library System. 14 Jan. 2008

[13] Energy Information Administration. http://www.eia.doe.gov/emeu/aer/txt/ptb0524.html. January 22, 2008.

[14] Energy Information Administration. http://tonto.eia.doe.gov/oog/info/twip/ twip.asp

[15] Harrison, George, and Starkey, Richard. "Photograph." *Ringo*. Apple Records, 1973.

Made in the USA
Middletown, DE
15 November 2014